Peoples and Nations of

AFRICA

A short history of
each country in Africa

Sheila Fairfield

DISCARD

HIRAM HALLE MEMORIAL

Pound Ridge, New York
10576

J
960
F

Gareth Stevens Publishing
Milwaukee

53597

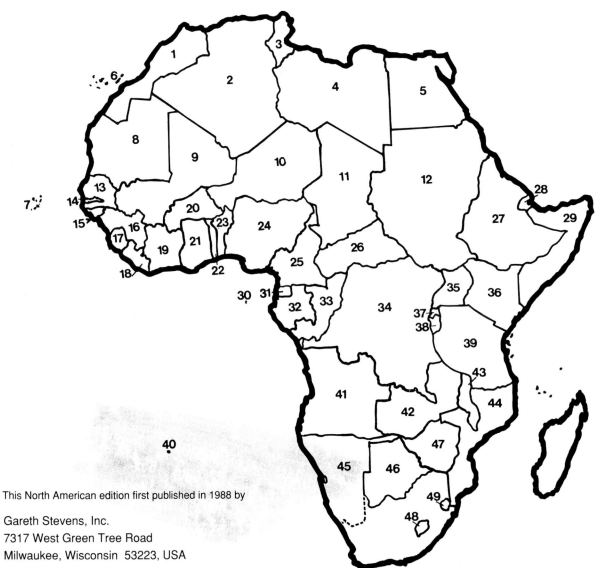

This North American edition first published in 1988 by

Gareth Stevens, Inc.
7317 West Green Tree Road
Milwaukee, Wisconsin 53223, USA

This fully edited US edition copyright © 1988. First published
in the United Kingdom with an original text copyright © 1987
by Young Library Ltd.

All rights reserved. No part of this book may be reproduced
or used in any form or by any means without permission in
writing from Gareth Stevens, Inc.

Designed by John Mitchell
Individual country maps by Denis Monham
   and Elizabeth O'Rourke
Full-continent map by Kate Kriege
Picture research by Sara Steel

1 2 3 4 5 6 7 8 9 94 93 92 91 90 89 88

Library of Congress Cataloging-in-Publication Data

Fairfield, Sheila.
  Peoples and nations of Africa.

  (Peoples and nations)
  Includes index.
  Summary: Presents a history of each nation of
Africa explaining the origins of the people and the
religion, language, culture, and migrations that
accompanied development towards nationhood.
  1. Africa — Juvenile literature. [1. Africa] I. Title. II.
Series: Fairfield, Sheila. Peoples and nations.
DT3.F3 1988 960   88-42922
ISBN 1-55532-903-9

CONTENTS

A note on the entries in this book: Each nation-state and dependency has a written entry and its own map or a reference to a map elsewhere in the book. Also, some countries include lands that are geographically separated from the main area. These lands do not have a separate entry but are included in the main country's entry. Finally, some countries are mentioned that are part of other continents. They do not have entries here, but you can find them in other volumes of the *Peoples and Nations* series.

GHANA

Ghana is a republic in West Africa, on the Gulf of Guinea. The modern state is named after an old empire that flourished in Mali and southern Mauritania in the Middle Ages. Modern Ghana is a group of small states. Those near the coast were known to Europeans as the Gold Coast.

The country has always been famous for gold. Merchants from Mali arrived around AD 1200, attracted by the gold fields. They settled in towns along the trade route from northwestern Ghana to Berekum. From there they traded with the Akan, a people who produced the gold in the southern forests and river valleys. The Malians spread through many small Akan states, introducing their Muslim religion as they went.

In the fifteenth century the Mossi people arrived in the north. They founded two kingdoms in northern Ghana. They were warlike riders from southwestern Niger, and their cavalry was strong enough to take land and trade from the Akan and the Mali merchants. The merchants then hired soldiers from their own country and took over one of the Akan states as a strong base from which to fight the Mossi.

There was continued fierce rivalry be-

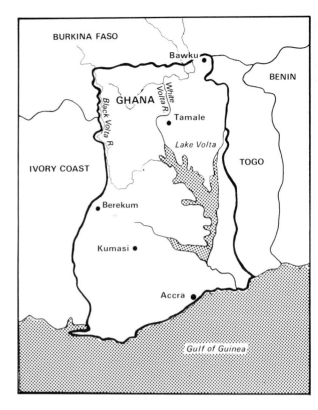

tween states, which became worse when Portuguese merchants arrived on the coast after 1470 looking for gold and slaves. The states had always traded in slaves, but here was a new, rich customer. Therefore, the slave trade led to constant warfare. The kings wanted to sell slaves because the price was good, but they could not always afford to part with any of their own people, who were busy producing other merchandise, such as gold. So the kings raided nearby kingdoms and sold the captives.

Eventually, the Portuguese merchants were replaced by British and Dutch merchants. During the eighteenth century they traded with a southern Akan people called

Cocoa is Ghana's biggest export. These farmers have just finished harvesting the pods from the cocoa trees.

This colorful festival in Ghana celebrated the yam, the most widely eaten vegetable in all Africa.

Fanti on the coast west of Accra, while east of Accra they dealt with the Ga and Adangbe.

Not all the states saw the Europeans as a source of profit. A group of inland Akan tribes hated them. Their kingdom, Ashanti, became the most powerful state in Ghana. In 1806-07 Ashanti warriors conquered the Fanti on the coast. This led to frequent troubles between Ashanti and Britain, especially when Britain turned against slavery and Ashanti still practiced it.

Britain began to control the Gold Coast in 1821, but not successfully, as the slave trade was gradually replaced by other trades. Although some coastal states came under strong British influence, British rule and Christian missions had little effect inland. Finally, however, there was another Ashanti war in 1901, after which most of modern Ghana was united as a British colony. British occupation now spread inland but had little influence on daily life.

Ghana became an independent country in 1857. Its boundaries have changed to include part of Togo to the east. English remains the official language.

IVORY COAST

This republic of thick forests lies on the Gulf of Guinea. Europeans called it the Ivory Coast because the forest elephants were hunted for their tusks.

There were, and still are, several different Negroid, or black African, groups: Agnis-Ashanti, Kroumen, Mande, and Baule, in particular. They farmed in the north and traded in gold, ivory, and nuts from the southern forest. At first their trade went north to the Malian empire, so Kong was an important base for Malian merchants and became a center for Malian ideas and Islam.

There were also many small states on the coast, and it was there that merchants from Europe came to buy ivory and slaves. The French set up a permanent trading post in 1842 and made the whole area a French protectorate in 1889.

As they settled the area, the French laid out cash-crop plantations and built the capital, Abidjan, in 1920. Roman Catholic Christianity arrived on the coast, but like the Muslim faith in the north, it remained the religion of a small group. Most of the people

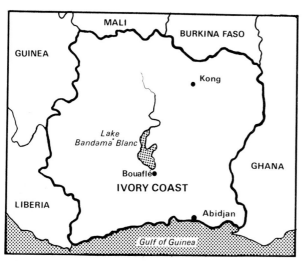

held to their traditional animist religions.

The country became independent in 1960, but has kept many links with France, including its language.

GUINEA

Guinea is a republic in West Africa, lying between Senegal and Sierra Leone. In early times there were native farming villages by the coast and small inland states set up by Susu and Mandingo people from Mali to the north. Some of these inland inhabitants were merchants, since they lived on the trade route between Mali and the coast. Still others were farmers. All maintained links with Mali and the upper Niger valley that the coastal people did not have. But Malian merchants eventually came down into Guinea to trade with the Europeans on the Guinean coast, because Mali had valuable trade along the Niger but no coastline.

At about the same time as the appearance of the Europeans (after 1440), a tribe of nomads arrived on the highlands of northern Guinea. They were the Fulani, from Tekrur in Senegal. They had been pagan, like the Susu and Mandingo, but were gradually being converted to Islam. The Guinean highlands were good pastureland for the Fulani cattle, so the tribe prospered and increased, and began to resent the controls and taxes which the local village chiefs tried to impose. The Fulani also felt they had more in common with Malian merchants, who were also Muslims and outsiders, than with their farming neighbors. In 1725 the Fulani, supported by the merchants, began a holy war against the non-Muslim people of Guinea and emerged as the strongest group.

The French gradually took control of the coastal trading towns, then spread inland. By 1893 Guinea was a French colony. Surprisingly, it was not the Fulani who made the fiercest resistance, but a Mande chief in eastern Guinea called Samori who held up the French advance for years.

French rule lasted until 1958, when Guinea became independent. Modern Guinea has not kept links with France, although the French language is one of nine main languages in use.

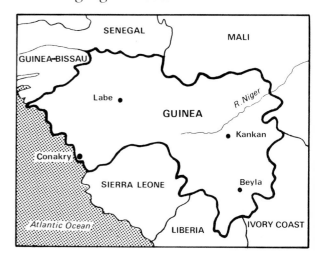

THE GAMBIA

The Gambia is a tiny country on the lower Gambia River. It is surrounded on three sides by Senegal, and the people are of the same stock.

From 1444 the Portuguese, French, Dutch, and British competed for trade on the coast, and Senegal eventually came under French control. In 1678 the British set up a trading post on James Island in the Gambia estuary, and their influence became the strongest in the land along the Gambia River.

Gambia finally became a British colony in 1888. The main center was Bathurst at the river mouth, but even this was not a big city. During the period of British rule there was trouble with warlike tribes that was only put down with the help of Senegal. When Gambia became independent in 1965 many people predicted that the same conflicts would happen again. They felt that Gambia depended on Senegal for survival, so the two countries ought to be joined. But Gambia remained independent and became a republic in 1970.

There were various proposals for closer ties. In 1982, the two countries formed a union called Senegambia. Under this scheme Gambia did not actually become part of

An advertisement for slaves. They were brought by ship from Gambia to work on rice plantations in the US.

GAMBIA NEGROES.

TO BE SOLD,
On TUESDAY, the 7th of June,
On board the SHIP
MENTOR,
Captain WILLIAM LYTTIETON,
Lying at MOTTE's wharf,

A Cargoe of 158 prime healthy young Negroes, juſt arrived in ſaid ſhip from the river Gambia, after a paſſage of 35 days.

The Negroes from this part of the coaſt of Africa, are well acquainted with the cultivation of rice, and are naturally induſtrious.

CONDITIONS of SALE.

To approved purchaſers, bonds payable the firſt of January, 1786, and to thoſe who make immediate payment in caſh, rice or any other produce, a proper diſcount will be made thereon.

ROBERT HAZLEHURST & Co.

No. 44. Bay.

Senegal, but the two countries now share armed forces, currency, and many government functions.

English is the official language.

BENIN

The small country of Benin on the Gulf of Guinea used to be called Dahomey. It lay inland from the tiny coastal states of the Ada people. In the far north was Bargu, a kingdom founded by people who claimed ancestry from beyond the Red Sea. Between Bargu and Dahomey and also on the coast, the Yoruba people of western Nigeria were active traders. After 1670 the Ada states fell into chaos because they were all competing for the slave trade with Euro-

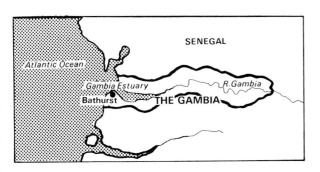

pean dealers. As the Ada kings grew weaker fighting the competition, the Europeans gained more control, and the Yoruba also profited from the decreased trade competition.

In 1724 Dahomey began to conquer the Ada states, to restore order, and to bring the slave trade under its own control. This led to war with the Yoruba. In the end, Dahomey held the coast except for Porto Novo, which was kept by the Yoruba and their Ada allies and became the center of their slave trade.

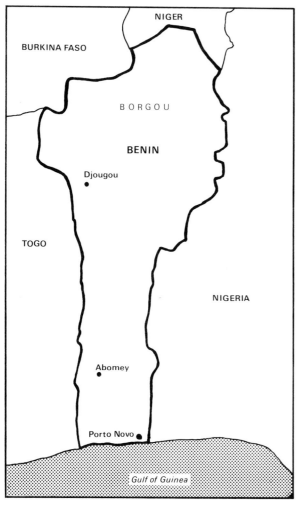

This small bronze statuette of a mounted warrior was made in Benin in the sixteenth century.

The British were active on the Nigerian coast to the east, although after 1818 they tried to stop the slave trade. This was difficult when Porto Novo, just next door but beyond their authority, was a flourishing slave port. The British, therefore, blockaded the whole coast, and the slave trade slowly died out.

At that time Europeans were trying to find other trades with West Africa. Usually they tried to control the states where they traded for fear of losing business through tribal wars or to rival European states. The

French began trading on the Dahomey coast, and by 1893 they had conquered the whole country. They used it as a route to their other colonies, further north. French rule lasted until 1960 and brought with it French law, language, education, and the Roman Catholic religion. The people had previously been animists.

In 1960 the colony became independent as one country and a republic. In 1975 it changed its name to Benin.

MALI

Mali is in West Africa. The southern part lies around the upper Niger River, where there has been a series of powerful kingdoms. The northern part is desert, where tribes of nomads have always lived.

The desert people are a mixture of Berbers and Bedouins, but are mainly Berbers. After the Bedouins came from Arabia around AD 1050, the Berbers adopted the Arabic language and have followed the Muslim religion since the eighth century.

Also in the eighth century a north African scholar reported a great kingdom in Mali called Ghana. This was quite different from modern Ghana. It actually lay in southwestern Mali and southeastern Mauritania. Some people think it was founded by Berbers, but before long it had been taken over by a black African people called the Soninke, or northern Mande, who lived by the Niger and skillfully farmed the land.

The kings of Ghana traded in gold. They controlled the buying of gold from people further south, while the Berbers controlled the merchant caravans that carried it north across the Sahara to be sold in

In Mali, as in many other parts of Africa, when there is something to be carried it is balanced on the head.

Morocco. The Ghanaian kings tried to take over the Saharan trade. At first the Berbers were unable to stop them, but in about 1050 their tribes came together in a powerful, militant Muslim group called the Almoravids, and they conquered Ghana in 1076. The Berbers knew little about agriculture or governing settled people. Therefore, their flocks ate up the pastures, and the crops died because the wells were neglected.

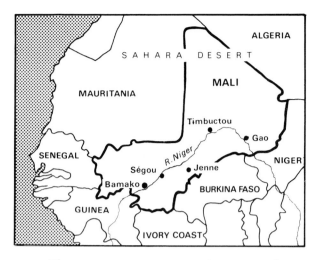

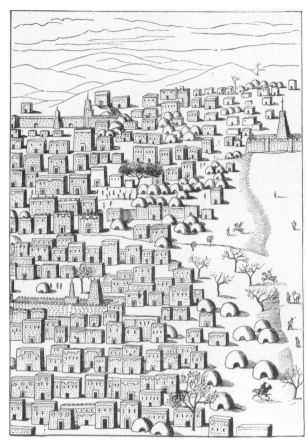

Two hundred years before this picture was drawn, Timbuktu was one of the greatest cities in Africa.

The next conquerors were southern Mande people called Keita. They took over the old kingdom of Ghana and made it into an enormous empire called Mali. Mali stretched from the Atlantic coast to the eastern corner of the modern Malian state. It was even richer than Ghana and was a center of Islamic learning.

Many of the ordinary people, however, were not Muslims. They held their old belief that a real king was one descended from godlike ancestors. They also shared this idea with the Songhai, a people to the southeast.

Like Ghana, Mali not only had rich trade across the desert, but also had another trade that was just as valuable down the Niger River. Fearing that the Songhai might move in on this trade, Mali conquered the Songhai people in about 1270. Once part of the Malian empire, however, the Songhai learned how it was run and how it could be overthrown. By 1400 they had won all the land east of Dejenne. They created a new empire which they ruled from their old capital of Gao. The Keita were now a smaller power, west of Dejenne.

In 1591 the area was invaded by an army from Morocco. The Songhai were driven eastward into modern Niger, while the Keita withdrew west to the country around Segou and built a prosperous farming kingdom. The Moroccan armies were left in control of Dejenne, Timbuktu, Gao, and the land in between, but when Morocco stopped supporting them their rule became very weak. During the eighteenth century desert Berbers took control once more.

The Berbers were not the ony nomadic shepherds in Mali. The Fulani were blacks from Senegal who wandered through West

Africa. They also were Muslims, and there were many of them in Segou. After 1800 they joined forces with the Tukulor in Senegal and launched a holy war.

By 1870 southern and western Mali were part of a Tukulor kingdom, where the people were Tukulor, Mande, and Fulani. The north and east were controlled by Berbers who had intermarried in the land around the Niger with the descendants of the Moroccan invaders. At that time the French were pressing inland from their colony in Senegal. They conquered Mali between 1881 and 1895, and it became part of French West Africa.

Mali became independent again in 1960 as a republic. There is still good farmland along the Niger, but the Sahara Desert is spreading southward, and modern Mali is threatened by drought.

GUINEA-BISSAU

Guinea-Bissau is a small country on the coast of West Africa that was settled by black farmers who lived in villages. Some were Malinke (Mandingo) who had come west from the inland empires of Mali.

While looking for trade, the Portuguese discovered that the coast had many inlets, creeks, and islands to shelter shipping. In the 1450s they built a fort at Cacheu which became their base for trading with local rulers. Bissau, another Portuguese port, is now the capital.

The area became the colony of Portuguese Guinea in 1879. By that time the coastal towns had a mixed population: Balante, Malinke, and other native merchants, and people of Portuguese and part-

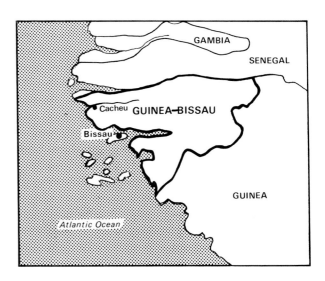

Portuguese descent. Inland were Fulani nomads. The Fulani and the Malian merchants brought in the Muslim religion, while the Portuguese brought Roman Catholic Christianity. Portuguese rule lasted until 1973, when Guinea-Bissau declared itself an independent republic.

Most people today are Balante, Malinke, and Fulani. About half are Muslims, while a few are Christians. Portuguese is the official language, but a dialect and local languages are generally spoken.

LIBERIA

Liberia is on the west coast of Africa. Most of the inland country was rain forest, where few people lived. Habitable land had groups of people like the Kru and Mande-speaking people from Mali.

Liberia was founded as a private colony for freed slaves. Although the United States did not abolish slavery until 1865, some US citizens disliked slavery and worked for its abolition long before then. In 1822 an antislavery society based in the US took land on the West African coast and founded a settlement for freed slaves which they called Monrovia.

The settlers of 1822 arrived from the US with plenty of ideas but little money. They had only the support of antislavery workers, and there was no strong government protecting them while they tried for a share of west coast trade. In 1847 they declared themselves the Republic of Liberia, hoping for foreign aid.

Several countries lent money, but the Liberians could not repay it. Therefore, the creditors had some monetary power and were able to influence the Liberian government. Still, no foreign country actually took control. The United States was growing stronger during the nineteenth century. Since the Liberians were of US origin, in time they persuaded the United States to protect them. Despite help from the US they were still a poor nation. Then in 1925 Liberia sold a US company the right to pro-

duce rubber from the trees of the rain forest. This kind of sale has made modern Liberia more prosperous. Foreign companies have since developed a rubber industry, metal and diamond mining, commercial fishing, and cash-crop farming.

English is the official language. Christianity is the dominant religion, although there are a number of Muslims.

SIERRA LEONE

Sierra Leone is a small republic on the coast of West Africa. The early settlers were groups of black African farmers. They were joined by Mande-speaking people from the Malian empire. Some of these were merchants who extended the Malian trade routes to the coast. Others were soldiers who fought their way along the coast in the sixteenth century to conquer a new home after the Malian empire had fallen. By that time the Portuguese had reached the coast.

Cattle farmers of Sierra Leone. The country was named by a Portuguese navigator. Its name means "Lion Mountain."

Other European explorers and traders followed, including the British.

From the 1780s public opinion in Europe turned against the slave trade. Therefore, in 1787 British reformers bought land on the coast of Sierra Leone that in 1792 became Freetown, a new settlement for freed slaves. The new settlers were a mixed bunch. Some had been rescued from captured slave ships. They could not go back to their own people, who had sold them, but were also not used to anything other than their own tribal life. Others had been born and brought up in Europe or the Americas. They were used to modern city life and tried to re-create it in Freetown. Many were Christians and brought their religion to Freetown, which became a center for missionary work in West Africa. In 1808 it became a British colony and a naval base for raids on slave ships.

The people inland were often hostile to this strange place on the coast, especially when Freetown citizens moved in on their profitable trades and influenced their customs and religion. In 1896 the whole country other than Freetown was placed under British protection.

This arrangement of a colony on the coast and a protectorate inland lasted until 1961. Then the two became independent as one country called Sierra Leone, which was the name given to it by the Portuguese. The official language is English, but local languages are widely spoken.

TOGO

Togo is a small republic in West Africa, with a short coastline on the Gulf of Guinea. The people of southern Togo are Ewe. They came from the Niger valley and settled in Togo in the fourteenth century. The people of northern Togo came from the basin of the Volta River in Ghana to the west and from Burkina Faso to the northwest.

The people on the coast traded in salt and slaves. African customers bought both, but when Europeans began trading they were chiefly interested in slaves. Togo became part of what the Europeans called the Slave Coast.

Slavery ended in the nineteenth cen-

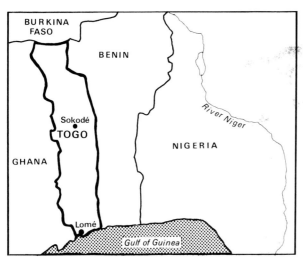

tury, but the Europeans remained and vied for any profitable business that might be had. In 1884 the Germans made treaties with coastal rulers and set up plantations. German interests spread, and in 1894 Togo became a German protectorate.

The Germans lost Togo during World War I, when the protectorate was divided between France and Britain. In 1956 the British part in the west voted to become part of Ghana, while the French part became an independent republic in 1960. French is still the official language, but local languages are spoken. Most people are animists, but about a third of Togo's people are either Christians or Muslims.

CHAD

Chad is a republic in North Africa. The south is watered by rivers and has fairly fertile land. The north is part of the Sahara Desert, so most of Chad suffers badly from drought and the danger of famine.

In the ninth century AD travelers discovered a state called Kanem in western Chad. The people, from the farming areas of the south, were Zaghawa nomads of the eastern Sahara. Zaghawa legends say that their earliest kings came from beyond the Red Sea in the sixth century.

Sometimes the state was strong enough to control other desert people or at least to share the valuable trade in salt and other things. Lake Chad was a convenient stopping place for trading caravans from Libya and Tunis. Through these northern traders the Muslim religion was brought into Kanem some time before 1200.

Kanem's power declined about 1500, and its trade was spoiled by desert raiders. In 1808 it was invaded by Muslims from Nigeria, but one of its own groups of nomads, the Kanembu, considered themselves just as worthy Muslims as the Nigerians. Therefore, they fought off the invasion and took over Kanem themselves. But they were not strong enough to repel the next invaders, the French, because Chad had no strong states outside Kanem. The French conquered Kanem, and by 1900 Chad was a French protectorate.

Chad was under French control until 1960, when it became an independent republic. It was now united as one country, which did not please the people of the north. Because of a threat of civil war, French soldiers stayed to keep order until 1965. When they left, civil war did break out and has continued ever since.

French is the official language, although Arabic is widely spoken, especially in the north, and there are many local languages. The main religions are Islam in the north and animism or Christianity in the south.

Mothers and children in the delta region of Senegal draw up goatskin water buckets from an ancient well.

SENEGAL

Senegal lies on the coast of West Africa. Its northern boundary, the Senegal River, has always been an important route to the interior. The Senegal valley has been known from earliest times as a source of gold.

The people who settled the valley were of black African stock. The Serer and Wolof lived in villages and were good at farming and crafts. Their society was organized in small chiefdoms. The Tukulor people had a kingdom called Tekrur which lay around the middle reaches of the Senegal River.

Many Fulani people lived in Tekrur. They were pagan nomadic shepherds who may have come from the Sahara Desert. Tekrur is thought to have been the first West African state to be converted to Islam. When Tekrur became a Muslim state some Fulani stayed, adopted the new religion, and took up a settled way of life. In time they became known as Tukulor. Other Fulani moved east with their herds, but in time they also took up the faith and became

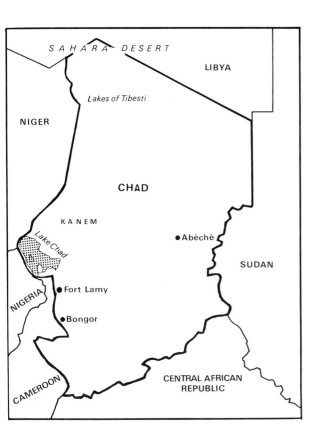

SAHARA DESERT

LIBYA

Lakes of Tibesti

NIGER

CHAD

KANEM

Lake Chad

•Abèchè

SUDAN

NIGERIA

•Fort Lamy

•Bongor

CAMEROON

CENTRAL AFRICAN REPUBLIC

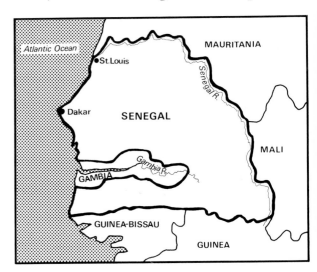

Melons, peppers, and other exotic fruits and vegetables are on sale in this Senegalese outdoor market.

called St. Louis, at the mouth of the Senegal River in 1659. By that time there were many ports with Wolof and Portuguese-Wolof merchants. However, during the eighteenth century the French slowly got control of trade on the coast north of the Gambia River, and the Portuguese were pushed

the most militant Muslims in West Africa.

In the seventeenth century the Tukulor conquered the region called Bonde in central Senegal. This was farmland, occupied by a Mande-speaking people.

In coastal Senegal the Wolof joined their small chiefdoms together into a powerful union, probably in the fourteenth century. The union impressed the Portuguese who arrived in 1445 to trade with the Wolof rulers for gold, slaves, and natural oils.

The French set up a trading post, later

further south, out of their own trade area.

In 1854 St. Louis became a French colony. From there the French explored upriver. They conquered the Tukulor lands and in 1864 established the port of Dakar. Dakar grew into a city of importance for trade and protection. The French made it the center of their empire in West Africa, which in time stretched across to Chad.

Senegal became an independent republic in 1960. It still has links with France, and French is its official language.

ALGERIA

Algeria, in northwestern Africa, stretches far inland from the Mediterranean coast into the Sahara Desert.

The original desert people were the Berbers and their language is still spoken. Tribes of Berber nomads grazed their herds in the inland hills and desert oases. They could grow some food crops at the oases, but were not skilled enough farmers to use the land that lay along the coast. However, they were skilled as desert raiders and often attacked travelers and the richer oases.

Arabs invaded North Africa from Arabia in the seventh century AD. They did not set up a state in Algeria, but they did bring their language and Islamic religion. The faith appealed to the Berbers, and many were converted. However, they still kept their independent ways and were soon arguing with the teaching of the Arabs. Eventually, different sects developed and set up little states of their own.

The Ibadite sect ruled from Wargla, an oasis in northern Algeria. From there a trans-Saharan trade route ran south. The Berbers controlled it and grew rich.

After 1050 more Arabs came, the Bedouins. They were desert people themselves, nomads and warriors. Mingling with the Berber tribes, the Bedouins became the Tuaregs of today.

Some Muslim Berber groups became very powerful. The Almoravids ruled western Algeria from 1082, and eastern Algeria was ruled by a group from Tunis. These were not rough desert raiders, but powerful sheiks. Similar rulers followed,

A nineteenth-century drawing of an Arab house in Algiers with carved wooden pillars and richly painted tiles.

but none succeeded in controlling the Berber or Bedouin tribes.

The next invaders were the Turks, in the sixteenth century. They were Muslims from Asia who were at war with European states. Therefore, they set up a naval base at Algiers from which they sent their fleet to fight the Spanish. But after losing the Battle of Lepanto in 1571 they gave up trying to attack Spain from Algiers. The Algerian captains were then left with no war to fight, and no good land to grow food. So they turned to raiding passing ships and became

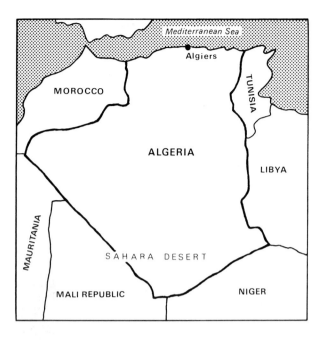

known as the Barbary, or Berber, Coast pirates. The plundered riches made Algiers a wealthy city.

In the eighteenth century European navies grew better at beating the pirates. When the sea captains could no longer bring in enough money to keep Algiers going, the people turned against their naval leadership. The original captains had brought soldiers from Turkey who had settled down with local wives. Their descendants still formed the army of Algiers, and in 1711 the people made the army commander, the Dey, their ruler. However, piracy continued, preventing Algiers from operating as an ordinary trading port. The Dey tried to tax the desert tribes without much success. The entire area was unruly.

In 1830 the French captured Algiers because they felt it was a source of trouble too close to home. Conquest of the inland areas took until 1879. Settlers were brought in to turn the coastal lands into good farmland.

Some were French, although many were Spanish, Italian, or Maltese.

At first the Algerians moved south into the hills and deserts, but many came back to the coast, and soon a big population of Algerian workers lived in towns and estates controlled by European settlers. This bred much discontent. Algerian resistance to French rule broke out in war in 1954. The fighting continued until 1962, when Algeria became an independent republic.

CAPE VERDE

Cape Verde is a group of islands in the Atlantic Ocean northwest of Senegal. There are ten main islands, but most people live on the islands of São Tiago, Santo Antão, São Vicente, and Fogo.

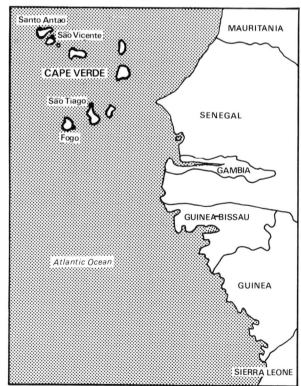

Two explorers from Portugal found Cape Verde in 1460. Portuguese settlers began to arrive in 1462. Portugal used the islands as a base for their West African trade, which included slaves. People from several countries of the West African mainland were sold as plantation workers for the settlers, but most of the slaves came from Gambia, Guinea, and Sierra Leone.

Some Portuguese settlers left Cape Verde to settle on the mainland. In time they formed a community in coastal cities that was part Portuguese and part African.

Cape Verde remained a plantation colony until 1974, when there was a revolution in Portugal that did away with colonial rule. Full independence as a republic came in 1975. Portuguese is still the official language, and the Roman Catholic religion that came with the Portuguese is still strong.

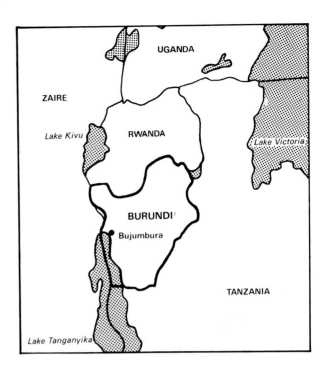

BURUNDI

Burundi is a small highland country at the north end of Lake Tanganyika. Before 1600 the Hutu people, Bantu-speaking black Africans, lived there as farmers. The Twa, a pygmy-like people, also lived in the area by hunting and gathering wild food.

Between 1300 and 1600 the Tutsi, a tall, pastoral people from the north, invaded. They established a kingdom in Burundi, as they had in Rwanda to the north. The Tutsi ruled the country and owned the cattle, while the Hutu went on farming as tenants, taxpayers, and managers of the farms.

In 1890 Burundi became part of German East Africa. However, the Germans lost it in World War I and after 1918 Burundi was governed by the Belgians. But the Tutsi kings remained on Burundi's throne with Belgian advisers.

During this European period, missionaries brought in the Roman Catholic religion. About half the people were converted from spirit worship, or animism.

Burundi became an independent kingdom again in 1962. In 1966 the Tutsi king was deposed and a republic declared. The Tutsi tried to win back the kingdom in 1972. There was fierce fighting and many were killed, but Burundi remained a republic. The language is a Bantu language, Kirundi.

TUNISIA

Tunisia is a small country with an important strategic position on the North African coast, because northern Tunisia overlooks the passage between the eastern and western halves of the Mediterranean Sea.

The early people were Berbers. At first they lived as nomads with herds of livestock. But after the arrival of Phoenicians in about 800 BC many of them settled down as farmers.

The Phoenicians came from what is now Lebanon and set up small supply ports on the northern coast. From there they could control the strait between Tunisia and Sicily. This control was important to them because the Greeks, their rivals in trade, had colonies in Sicily.

A girl dressed in the colorful traditional costume of the Kairouan district of northern Tunisia.

The ports had a great effect on the life of the Berbers. Some Berbers moved to the coast and began to grow crops to sell to the townspeople. Others would cross the Sahara, steal or buy valuable goods, and bring them back to sell to Phoenician merchants.

By about 600 BC one of the towns, Carthage, had become a great city. Carthage, which stood near modern Tunis, became the center of a Mediterranean empire which lasted until its conquest by the Romans in 146 BC. The Romans made the region a province and called it "Africa." Carthage also became a center of learning and reli-

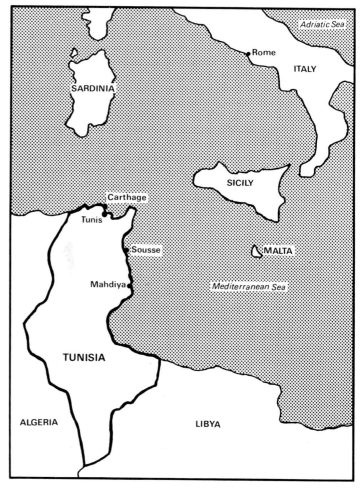

In the Monastir region of Tunisia young women perform a folk dance against a background of date palms.

gious teaching, because Jewish merchants and refugees settled there and brought their faith, Judaism. Christianity also flourished there after AD 300.

The Arabs conquered the province of Africa, which they called "Ifriqiya," between AD 670 and 702. They brought their own Muslim religion. The Berbers valued the Muslim faith and Arab learning, but soon rebelled against Arab government. Then, various Berber Muslim chiefs became rulers of Ifriqiya, but each in turn was ousted by another. During the eleventh century more desert warriors, the Bedouins from Arabia, arrived. Chaos followed. Ifriqiya and its civilization shrank to a tiny area around Mahdiya.

The Turks invaded in the sixteenth century, and Tunisia became part of the huge Turkish Empire. The new invaders were also Muslims, but their empire included many nationalities. Tunis became more of a mixture than ever. The Turks' control of Tunisia was never firm. They had no influence at all over the Berbers and Bedouins.

In 1830 the French began an occupation of Algeria, Tunisia's western neighbor. The French felt their Algerian colony would be safer if they also controlled Tunisia. At that time Tunisia was governed by a Bey on behalf of the Turks. The Bey hoped to get loans and technical help from the French without losing his independence. But in 1881 Tunisia became a French protectorate. The Bey still governed but the French made the decisions.

The French invested in mining and agriculture. French, Italian, and Maltese settlers came to work new farms. French education was introduced, and soon there was a new generation of well-educated Tunisians dissatisfied with French control and the Bey's government. Therefore, Tunisia pushed for and became a fully independent republic in 1957. Most modern Tunisians are Muslims, and they speak Arabic and French.

MOROCCO

Morocco, in northwestern Africa, has a long coastline facing the Atlantic Ocean and a short one facing the Mediterranean Sea. Inland there is a plain, and behind the plain are mountains and desert.

The plain is fertile and can support a rich civilization. The Phoenicians discovered this in the eighth century BC and founded the town of Larache. In time this became part of an empire ruled from another Phoenician city, Carthage, in Tunisia. When Rome conquered Carthage, the plains of Morocco also became Roman. In turn the Romans were ousted by the Arabs, who were in Morocco by AD 700. Under all these rulers the plain and its cities were rich and developed. Art flourished, as well as business. There was a highly civilized life and an organized government.

The mountains and deserts were a different world. Here lived the Berbers, tribes of nomadic shepherds. They had a hard life. The only thing they had in common with the plains people was religion. The Arabs brought in the Muslim faith, and many Berbers were converted. The Berbers then divided into different sects which competed with each other. They tried, many times, to take over the vast plain and all its wealth.

Berber chiefs who conquered cities were always changed by their new life. The chiefs became softened by civilization, but they also found that they had to rule their new subjects harshly to keep control of a complicated city society. But as each chief's harsh rule increased, his people no longer remained loyal. Without support from his

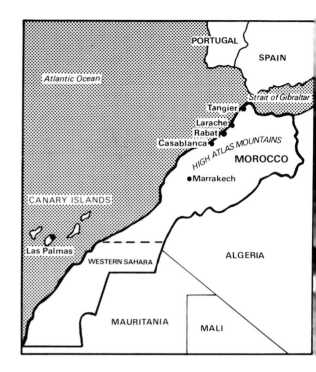

subjects, he would then be overthrown by another Berber chief hungry for power.

In 1082 one Berber group, the Almoravids, succeeded in conquering and uniting all Morocco, as well as part of Spain. They protected their kingdom through fortified cities between the plain and the desert. The Arabic culture of the cities survived.

At about that time, the Bedouins from Arabia appeared in the desert. The lives of the Bedouins and Berbers were so similar that they mingled and became one people in time. Only in the High Atlas Mountains did Berber stock remain pure. Even though the cities had an Arabic civilization, the arrival of Arabs in the desert did nothing to bring the desert and the plain together.

The political contact with Spain changed after 1415. Muslim rulers in Spain were driven back into Morocco, and Christian Spanish and Portuguese kings captured towns on the Moroccan coast. However, Morocco remained strong and rich enough to keep out any further European invasion until the twentieth century.

In 1894 a sultan came to the throne who wanted to modernize Morocco. He tried to force European ideas on Moroccans who did not want them. This led to civil war. At that time the French held Algeria to the east and the Spanish held land south of Morocco. Both countries wanted to stop the fighting in Morocco in case it spread to their own colonies. They also wanted the Moroccan city of Tangier and the Strait of Gibraltar in their own hands for defensive reasons. In 1912 Tangier was made an international zone. Most of Morocco became a French protectorate, but southern Morocco became a Spanish protectorate.

The French built up a potash-mining industry, and a new industrial society grew up on the coast in big port cities like Casablanca. Morocco became independent again in 1956. It still has rich agricultural land and a mainly Muslim population. Arabic is the official language, but Berber, French, and Spanish are spoken too.

In southern Morocco is a long-disputed region known as Western Sahara. The area was a Spanish protectorate between 1884 and 1975. Morocco and Mauritania have fought over the territory.

The people of Western Sahara have been Arab in lifestyle, language, and religion since the Middle Ages, and want independence. On the coast there is another kind of life, because Spain built up a mineral industry and towns grew up to serve it. Morocco holds the towns and the coast, while desert guerrillas hold the rest.

BURKINA FASO

Burkina Faso is in West Africa, south of the great bend in the upper Niger River. It contains the source of the Volta River. The first settlers were black African farmers living in villages, each with its own chief.

To the north lay the empire of Mali. Merchants from Mali used to travel south from Djenne to Bobo-Dioulasso, where they founded a trading colony after AD 1200. This was near the gold fields of the Black Volta valley. The merchants also brought their

There is not much money for education in Burkina Faso. These children use little black-boards instead of paper.

The animal which decorates this chief's home in Burkina Faso is the leopard, known throughout most of Africa.

Muslim religion, which spread along the trade routes.

The Mali empire was often attacked by the Mossi people, warlike bands of horsemen who had settled in southwest Niger. During the fifteenth century many Mossi moved west. They could not conquer Mali or the empire of the Songhai people that followed it, but they did overrun the farming people around the Volta River. There they stayed, unable to go farther north, living on tribute from the villages. In time the Mossi blended with the village people and adopted the local tribal religions.

There were two Mossi kingdoms: Yatenga in the north and Ouagadougou in the south. They were both strong enough to survive until about 1900, when they were conquered by the French.

The French ruled Senegal to the west and wanted to extend their power east. So in 1919 they made the Mossi states into a colony called Upper Volta. In 1960 Upper Volta became an independent republic, and its name was changed to Burkina Faso in 1984. French is the official language, but many local languages and dialects are spoken. Most of the people are animists, but about one-third are Muslims.

MAURITANIA

Mauritania is in West Africa, where the Sahara Desert reaches the Atlantic. The only fertile land lies along the Senegal River, which forms the southwestern boundary.

Most of Mauritania is desert, but it was not always so. There used to be wide areas of rough grazing land where tribes of nomadic shepherds lived. At first they were Berbers, like the people of Libya and Algeria, but after AD 1050 there were also Bedouins from Arabia. In time, the Berbers of Mauritania were absorbed by the Bedouins and adopted their language and Muslim religion. The southeast was once part of the Ghana kingdom (see page 9). In the southwest is the valley of the Senegal River. This attracted black farmers who made a settled society there and adopted Islam.

During the seventeenth century the

In the ancient Mauritanian city of Chinguetti stands a stone minaret built in the twelfth century.

French explored the coast of West Africa looking for trading bases. In about 1640 they built a town at the mouth of the Senegal. During the next 200 years they concentrated on the fertile riverside strip and on the country south of the river, which became a French colony. French control eventually spread across the whole of Mauritania, but that was not until 1903. French customs, language, and education could then be found in towns like Nouakchott on the coast and in the settled area along the Senegal, but the French state had little effect on the desert people. In 1960 Mauritania became an independent republic. Most of the people are Muslims. Their languages are Arabic and French.

The Turks ruled Libya when this picture was drawn in 1832. It shows the defensive walls of Tripoli Harbor.

LIBYA

Libya, which lies on the northern coast of Africa, has three areas: Cyrenaica, Tripolitania, and Fezzan.

Cyrenaica is a plateau in eastern Libya, running back from the coast into the desert. In 630 BC Greeks from the island of Thera settled on the coast, founded a town called Cyrene (modern Shahhat), then spread inland to farm the fertile valleys.

Tripolitania is in western Libya. It was settled by the Greeks' great rivals, the Phoenicians, who came from Lebanon. They were long-distance traders and founded ports on the Tripolitanian coast where their ships could be supplied and repaired. The native people were desert nomads. The Greeks called them Libyans, and later the Arabs called them Berbers. Anything they could buy or steal from neighbors and travelers they took to the coast to sell to the Phoenicians. Some also settled around the coastal towns where the land was fertile and grew food to sell to the trading fleets. Tripolitania's coast became rich through a busy trade economy.

Fezzan lies inland from Tripolitania. It is desert with oases where palm trees grow and gardens can be cultivated. The Fezzan was peopled by Berber tribes including the Garamantes, who were famous raiders. None of Libya's early rulers ever controlled the Fezzan.

Tripolitania and Cyrenaica were ruled by Rome after 146 BC, and Tripolitania became one of the Roman Empire's main sources of grain and olives.

In AD 647 the Arabs conquered the coast and introduced their Muslim faith. Many Berbers were converted, and some Berber chiefs went on to become powerful Muslim rulers themselves. Therefore, the Arabs feared that their hold on Libya might be

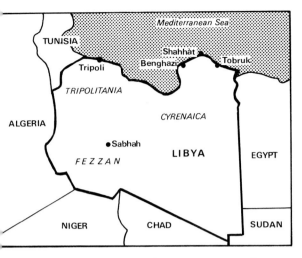

threatened. In 1050 they sent in Bedouins from Arabia to deal with the rebellious chiefs. In time these desert warriors spread throughout the deserts of North Africa.

By 1230 Tripolitania was part of a Berber Muslim state ruled from Tunisia. Cyrenaica was officially ruled from Egypt, but in fact it was run by the Bedouins.

In the sixteenth century there was an invasion from Turkey. Tripolitania and Cyrenaica remained part of the Turkish empire until 1911, but there were times when Turkish rule was very weak, and a local family held the real power. Although the Turks were Muslims like the Arabs, they never controlled the Fezzan.

In 1911 Italy invaded Libya and held it until World War II. By that time Libya was a mixture of Berber, Bedouin, and Turkish people, with descendants of several Mediterranean nations living in the coastal towns. In 1951 the country became independent as a federation of three provinces. The Bedouin sheik who ruled Cyrenaica was installed as king.

In 1959 the Libyans discovered oil, making it possible for the whole country to be rich. But there were arguments about how to use the money and about Libya's dependence on foreign oil companies. In 1969 the king was deposed. Since then, Libya has become an Islamic state.

NIGERIA

Nigeria has a coastline on the Gulf of Guinea with many river mouths, creeks, inlets, and marshes. The Niger River flows down to this coast through western Nigeria, and the Benue River flows through the east.

Inland there is forest and a mixture of highland and valley, pasture, crop land, and savanna grassland giving way to desert scrub in the north. A variety of people have inhabited Nigeria. The Hausa people live in the north, the Yoruba in the west, and the Ibo in the east.

The Hausa are a Negroid, or black African, people with a language of North African origin. They are a settled people using agriculture to develop their land and trade to enrich it. Hausa kingdoms in

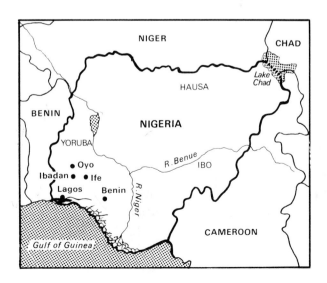

northern Nigeria traded with the Mali and Songhai empires to the west, and through this contact the Muslim religion reached them. Many Hausa merchants and rulers were converted, but their pagan beliefs survived as well. Trade with Mali ceased after 1591 because of war in Mali itself. But there was still valuable trade to be had across the Sahara. Since the merchants' route came down from Tunisia and Tripolitania, and Hausaland lay at its southern end, the Hausa kingdoms prospered.

The Yoruba people had kingdoms in western Nigeria. They are black Africans with a West African language. They have always liked living in towns, and their first important town was Ife, which they founded in about AD 1000. It is said that a prince of Ife founded the later city of Benin some time after AD 1200. In the seventeenth century the town of Oyo became the center of a Yoruba empire. Yoruba soldiers were famous cavalrymen, and Yoruba people conquered land far to the south and west.

The Ibo people have always been known

Three faces of Nigeria. The two young women, one in modern dress and the other more traditional, have scars on their faces. They were cut in babyhood purely for decoration. The man is a Hausa Muslim from northern Nigeria.

as traders, moving about the network of waterways in southeastern Nigeria. They did not have kingdoms; rather, their idea of power was an efficient business system.

Another important group in Nigeria were the Fulani, a nomadic black African people who had moved through West Africa for generations. They mixed with Berber and Arab nomads and were impressed by the strict religious teaching of the desert holy men. On the other hand, the Hausa Muslims were not as strict and many people in Nigeria were pagan. In the early nineteenth century the Nigerian Fulani began a holy war to enforce their beliefs. They conquered much of northern Nigeria and in 1817 conquered the northern Yoruba. This caused great upheaval in Yorubaland since people fled from the war areas to settle further south. New cities grew up, of which

Ibadan was one. Yoruba merchants started to build a new economy that did not depend on business on the West African coasts. They had two motives: first, to get as much of the trade in palm oil, ivory, and gold as they could; and second, to stop the slave trade now that European public opinion was against it.

The British traded with the Ibo and the Yoruba and explored up the Niger to make contact with the Fulani-ruled Hausa states in the north. In 1851 they deposed the king of Lagos for slaving and made Lagos a British colony. The Ibo and the Yoruba fought over the European trade, but there was also violent disagreement as to whether the British presence was a source of profit or of trouble.

From 1885 much of southern Nigeria was a British protectorate. The British conquered the east and north by 1906, but their impact was always greater in the south.

When British rule ended in 1960 a federation was formed of three regions: the old territories of the Hausa, Yoruba, and Ibo. In modern Nigeria these regions are divided into many provinces, but their old character remains. One exception, however, is in the east. When oil was discovered in the southeast in 1956-57, the Ibo tried to break from the federation in 1966-67, and civil war broke out.

Modern Nigeria has many big cities in the south. Overseas trade is still important, especially in oil. English is the official language but the dominant spoken languages are Hausa, Yoruba, and Ibo. The north is Muslim, while the people of the south are Christian or animist.

SUDAN

The Sudan is a republic in northeast Africa. Much of the country is desert, although central and southeastern Sudan has fertile land around the rivers of the White Nile, Blue Nile, and Atbara. Darfur, in the west, is the fringe of the Sahara. The Sudd in the southeast is marshland.

Some of the Sudanese are Nile Valley people who have always lived along the river, or who moved south from Egypt. There are also Negroid, or black African, people who moved into Sudan from the west, across the countries south of the Sahara. Others, like the Luo, came north from Ethiopia. Most Sudanese of today, especially in central Sudan, are Arabs.

The earliest people were the Nubians. They lived in northern Sudan and what is now southern Egypt. Before 1050 BC their country was invaded by the Egyptians, who

established trading posts along the Nile, but Egypt lost control, and the area became the independent kingdom of Kush.

The kings of Kush kept the Egyptian style of government. From about 750 BC they were strong enough to control Egypt as well, until they were driven back by an invasion of Assyrians from Asia. The Assyrians had learned how to make weapons out of iron, and during the invasion the kings of Kush found out, to their cost, how effective these could be. The Kush then moved out of northern Sudan and a long way upriver to a place where there was iron ore and enough timber to fuel the smelting furnaces. There they began producing iron for themselves, at a safe distance from Egypt. Their new capital was Meroe, near modern Shendi. Their kingdom came to be called Meroe, too, and remained powerful for centuries. Meroe was a place where people from south of the Sahara came into contact with the Nile Valley and with ideas from the Mediterranean world. Other ideas also came in from the east, for the Kush had ports on the Red Sea.

After the fall of Meroe, there were three small kingdoms in Sudan. In the sixth century AD they were converted to Christianity by missionaries from Egypt. When the Arabs invaded Egypt in AD 639 they could not conquer these kingdoms, but they did make treaties with them which allowed trade. They also brought the Bedouins into Egypt, and these nomads wandered into the deserts of the Sudan. The Arab merchants and the Bedouins both slowly established Islam in Sudan. When the Christian kingdoms collapsed, they were replaced by many small units under local sheiks. Many of these, if not all, owed some kind of allegiance to Egypt.

In the south things were different, because the Muslim faith did not spread so far. In about AD 1500 kingdoms were set up by the Luo and by the Funj. The Luo came originally from southwestern Ethiopia. Their kingdom, called Shilluk, lay north of the point where the White Nile joins the Sobat River. The Funj had their capital at Sennar on the Blue Nile. No one is sure where they came from, but it may have been from further upriver. The Funj and the Luo followed their own religions, as did the various small groups in the far south.

During the 1820s Egypt invaded Sudan again and took control of the whole country by 1875. However, in 1881 a Sudanese Muslim cleric called Muhammed Ahmed led an uprising against Egyptian rule. He was believed to be the *Mahdi*, or messiah, sent by God to save his people. The Sudan was independent again by 1885.

By that time the British controlled Egypt. Like all Egyptian rulers they worried about what would happen if any enemy controlled the upper waters of the Nile. They reconquered the Sudan, which was ruled as Anglo-Egyptian Sudan until 1956.

In 1956 Sudan became a united country and an independent republic. Arabic is the official language, but English is widely spoken.

RWANDA

Rwanda is a small republic lying north of Burundi and sharing much of its history. The people are mainly Bantu-speaking blacks called Hutu. They were invaded

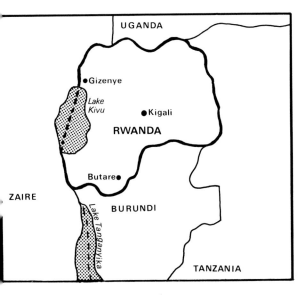

GABON

Gabon is a republic on the west coast of central Africa. Most of the country is tropi-

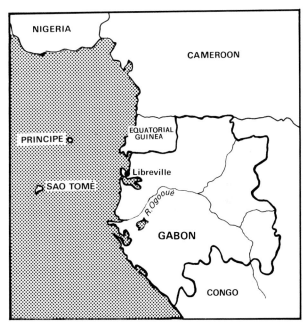

about AD 1600 by the Tutsi, an aristocratic tribe of cattle owners from the north. The Tutsi established a kingdom in Rwanda which survived even an occupation by Germans in 1890.

The Germans controlled Tanganyika and wanted to extend their influence to Lake Kivu. They held all of Rwanda until World War I, after which it was governed by Belgium. It remained a kingdom, but it was ruled on Belgian advice.

In 1959 there was a revolution in which the Hutu destroyed the Tutsi monarchy and killed many Tutsi. They declared a republic, which the Belgians agreed to in 1961. Rwanda became fully independent in 1962.

The language is Kinyarwanda. Swahili is also spoken, expecially in the towns, as is the Belgian version of French. Most people are animist.

cal forest. The people are black African and Bantu-speaking. South of the River Ogooue they are mainly Eshira in the southwest and Adouma in the southeast. North of the river they are mainly Fang.

After 1470 the Portuguese came to the coastal villages and the nearby islands of São Tomé and Principe. They wanted trade and slaves for the island plantations, but they never tried to control Gabon.

In 1839 the French leased land on the coast, and by 1849 they had founded there the town of Libreville as a refuge for freed slaves. The new settlers came from various West African countries. Many had been rescued from slaving ships by the French navy.

Libreville needed support if it was to succeed. The French wanted to protect it from inland tribes of Gabon and to make an income from the surrounding country. They explored upriver and into the forests and slowly came to rule the whole of Gabon, although they did not defeat the Fang until 1911.

The French found valuable minerals, timber, and rubber. Their rule ended in 1960. Gabon is now independent and still prosperous. French is the official language. While many people in the coastal areas belong to the Roman Catholic Church, the majority follow local animist faiths.

NIGER

Niger is a large, mostly desert country in the middle of North Africa. Only the south and southwest have always been well watered and suitable for growing crops.

The Hausa are a black African people who settled in southern Niger. Their language belongs to the same group as that of ancient Egypt and the Berber languages of North Africa. They lived as farmers and merchants, but there was never enough good land to allow them to build great kingdoms, as they did in Nigeria.

The Songhai, a black African people who were originally farmers and fishers, came from an area called Dendi in southwest Niger. From there they conquered an empire big enough to include much of Mali. When the empire itself was conquered in 1591, they were left with Dendi and made it their home.

Both Songhai and Hausa had their own religions. After AD 1200, however, many of them, particularly among the Hausa, were converted to the Muslim faith which came into Niger from Mali in the west and across the desert to the north.

Between the farmlands of the south and the northern desert there was once a large area of grazing land used by Berber desert nomads. Another Muslim nomadic people, the Fulani, also lived there. They were blacks from Senegal who had spread out over West Africa with their herds.

There was no government over the

The millet harvest is over. The strange-looking mud buildings on the left are used to store the grain.

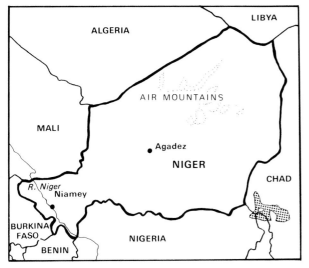

A Theban tomb painting of a nobleman and his wife at table about 4,000 years ago.

whole country until the French invaded in the late nineteenth century. The French knew that there had always been valuable minerals in the Air Mountains of northern Niger, and they were hoping to find more. While Niger was under French control, uranium was discovered. This mineral was so valuable that it provided enough money to support Niger as an independent state. The French left in 1960. French is the official language, but Hausa and local languages are spoken.

In recent years the grazing lands of mid-Niger have been slowly swallowed by the desert, although there is still farming in southern Niger.

THE CANARY ISLANDS

These seven islands lie off the northwestern coast of Africa (see map of Morocco on page 22). They are part of Spain and the people are mainly of Spanish descent. The people make their living mainly from tourism. The islands are Tenerife, La Palma, Gomera, Hierro, Gran Canaria, Lanzarote, and Fuerteventura.

EGYPT

Egypt is in northeastern Africa. The valley of the Nile River runs through it from south to north. Most Egyptians live along the river where the land is fertile, since on either side of the Nile Valley is desert.

Early Egyptians saw the valley as two places: Upper and Lower Egypt. Lower Egypt was around the Nile delta where the river splits into many streams. There were water meadows and gardens with good

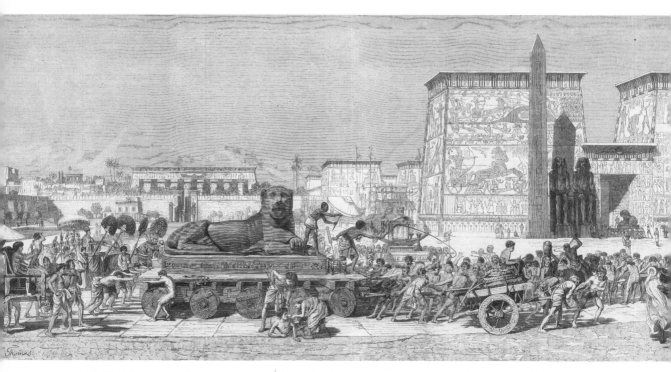

rainfall. The people were in touch with the Mediterranean world through their busy ports. On the other hand Upper Egypt lay between the delta and Aswan. Here there was little rain but the annual flooding of the Nile made the land rich. The people were as prosperous as those of Lower Egypt, but they took less interest in the Mediterranean world. They were also cut off from the Red Sea coast by desert.

In 3200 BC Upper and Lower Egypt were united under one king, or pharaoh, with an elaborate government. The pharaoh was regarded as the link between gods and humans.

The united Egypt was rich and powerful for centuries. The great pyramids and other monuments were built for the pharaohs. But the people always remembered their original two lands. Whenever the pharaohs were weak or enemies caused trouble,

Egypt returned to its old divided state.

After 1574 BC, in the period called the New Kingdom, the pharaohs were strong enough to withstand any attack. But at last, in 525 BC, Egypt was conquered and became part of the Persian empire.

The ports of the Nile delta still attracted foreign merchants who wanted not only Egyptian goods but luxuries shipped up the Red Sea from the east. The most important of these merchants were the Greeks, who settled in the delta in large numbers.

Greek influence grew stronger, until in 332 BC the Greek king, Alexander the Great, conquered Egypt. From then on, the division between the two Egypts was clearer than ever. Upper Egypt had a truly Egyptian people speaking their own language and farming the river valley. Lower Egypt was like Greece, and its capital, Alexandria, was like a Greek city. When Christianity came,

The great stone statue on the left is being hauled by Israelite slaves into position at an ancient Egyptian temple.

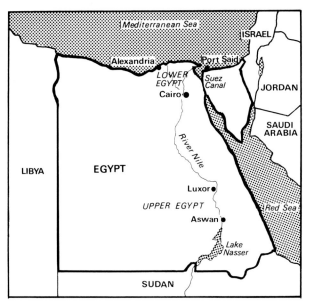

it spread in two forms. Lower Egypt adopted the Greek Orthodox faith, while Upper Egypt adopted the Coptic faith, with quite different beliefs about the nature of Christ.

Nomads lived in the eastern and western deserts. They held to beliefs of their own until they were converted by later invaders, the Arabs, who invaded in AD 639. They established the Arabic language and its literature and the Muslim faith. They ruled Egypt well until their empire became too big to hold together. Then soldiers, many of them non-Arab slaves who had been captured in battle, became Egypt's ruling class. Even when the Turks conquered Egypt in 1517 this class, called Mamelukes, went on running the country for its new masters.

The Turkish empire was enormous. It included people of many nationalities, and by 1800 many of these had settled in Egypt, joining the original Nile valley farmers and the Arab desert tribes who had come in under Arab rule.

In 1805 Muhammad Ali, an army officer from the Turkish colony of Albania, became ruler of all Egypt. He wanted to extend Egypt's power up the Nile, since the whole country depended on the river. He built up a strong army and conquered the Sudan. He also wanted Egypt to be a modern state, so he enlisted the help of European countries. After his death, however, Europeans won control of Egypt altogether and of the Suez Canal, which had been cut to link the Mediterranean with the Red Sea. The Egyptian government was in debt to Britain and had to sell its shares in the canal to the British government. Britain then controlled Egypt to make sure that nothing happened to the canal, which was now the main route to British colonies in the East.

Egypt became an independent kingdom again in 1922. The British agreed to leave the country except for the canal area by 1936, but World War II caused them to stay longer. By 1952 the Egyptians were very discontented with British influence and with their king, Farouk. Both were overthrown and Egypt became an independent republic.

Egypt has lost some of its western desert to Libya, and the northeastern frontiers have changed because of wars — and subsequent treaties — with Israel. Egypt gave up the Sudan in 1953-56.

ETHIOPIA

Ethiopia is a mountainous country in northern East Africa. The Blue Nile rises in Lake Tana. The first major settlements were on the Red Sea coast. By AD 100 a kingdom called Axum arose in what is now Eritrea. The people were Jews, Arabs, and Africans of the northeastern coast. Their port was Adulis, and they became rich on its trade.

Greek merchants from Egypt were active on the Red Sea. They used Adulis as a base and brought Greek ideas to add to the Jewish-Arab-African mixture. The Greeks' main Egyptian city, Alexandria, was a center of Christian teaching. From there the merchants brought their Greek Orthodox Christianity to Axum. At the same time, Egyptian Coptic missionaries heard about this Red Sea kingdom where their merchant neighbors went. It was the Coptic faith that lasted in Axum, but the people blended it with their own Jewish or pagan beliefs.

After AD 650 there was a new power in Egypt and the Red Sea — Islam. Strong Islamic Arab rulers took most of Axum's trade and conquered Egypt.

Since the rulers of Axum were poorer than the Arabs and isolated, they moved inland and settled in the mountains around Lake Tana, where they developed a farming kingdom. Their own language slowly gave way to local Amharic. The coastal region became a group of small Muslim states.

The inland Christian kingdom of Ethiopia no longer had control over the coast, but neither could the coastal Muslims conquer it. They had to spread their influence around the Christian kingdom. Harar, now in southern Ethiopia, became a Muslim cen-

On the right, oxen draw a primitive wooden plow through dry and stony Ethiopian soil.

ter. From there Islam spread inland and reached the Sidama in the southwest.

The Sidama belonged to a group of peoples native to northern East Africa and resembled the African people of Axum. They were farmers and lived in small kingdoms. North of them were the Luo, who could be warriors, nomads, or settlers, according to chance. Not all Sidama became Muslims. Some of them and most of the Luo had religions of their own.

Eventually Europeans heard about the Christian kingdom surrounded by Muslim or pagan states. The Portuguese first visited Ethiopia in the 1490s, and in 1543 they helped defeat a Muslim attack. For a time it seemed as if European ideas would take root, but the Portuguese tried to teach their own Roman Catholicism and were thrown out in 1648.

Other foreigners were not thrown out so easily. The Galla were pagan nomads from

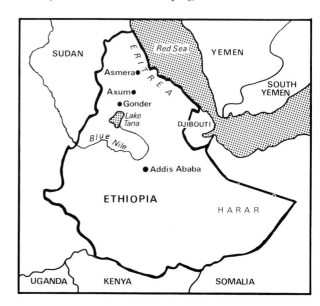

Somalia who had been moving into southern Ethiopia for years in large numbers and who broke up the settled farming life wherever they went.

By 1800 Ethiopian rulers had little authority left and no outside allies. At the same time European countries were trying for power on the Red Sea coast. Britain, France, and Italy all had interests there.

In 1855 a warlord called Ras Kasa broke away from the tradition of "Ethiopia alone" and used European help to beat the Galla. He became the Emperor Theodore, ruling in the north. In the south, King Menelik reigned over a people who included Galla and Somali. In 1889 he used Italian help to win the throne and joined north and south into a new, bigger Ethiopia.

The Italians went on to conquer Eritrea, as Axum was then called. In 1896 they tried to conquer Menelik, but he defeated them.

Italy tried again in 1936 and won but later lost Ethiopia during World War II.

After the war Eritrea was still a separate place, but in 1952 the area was linked with Ethiopia. Ethiopia saw Eritrea as its own earliest territory and only coast, so the link became a takeover. But Eritrea had not had any real tie with Ethiopia since about AD 700. The people were quite different and wanted to be independent. There are Tigre-speaking Christians in the inland hills, Tigre-speaking Muslims on the northern coast and western lowlands, and Muslim Danakil nomads in the south. There has been war over Eritrean independence for years.

In 1974 a revolution in Ethiopia deposed the emperor, Haile Selassie, and a Marxist government took power. The war for independence goes on, made worse by long periods of drought and famine.

SOMALIA

Somalia is a desert country in northeastern Africa. The coast forms a cape along the southern shore of the Gulf of Aden.

The Somali coast has always been a trading place for merchant ships in the Indian Ocean. Egyptians, Greeks, and Arabs all came down through the Red Sea and settled as businessmen in Mogadishu and other coastal towns. The Arabs were dominant from the seventh century AD, and the coast became strongly Muslim. Zeila was an important base from which Arab ideas spread far inland.

Bantu speakers also settled on the coast. They had little in common with the people of the interior, the Galla and Somali. Their language was Swahili, their life was urban, and they therefore fitted into the Arabs' trading world.

Galla and Somali tribes are nomads who are found in Somalia and elsewhere. Their languages are Cushitic. Somalia is very dry, and the nomads have to travel long distances for seasonal rainfall and fresh grazing. There have been long disputes and sometimes war over this migration. Somali and Galla shepherds range over parts of Kenya, Ethiopia, and Djibouti. The governments of these countries then try to claim them as subjects. The government of Somalia, on the other hand, tries to claim the foreign ranges as part of Somalia, because there are Somali people using them. Whenever there is serious drought the disputes get worse, because the herds have to travel farther.

Britain held most of northern Somalia as a protectorate from the 1880s. Italy held the coast from 1889 until 1941. The interior nomads never took the slightest notice of either government.

The two areas were brought together as an independent republic in 1960. Somali is the official language, but Arabic, Italian, and English are also spoken.

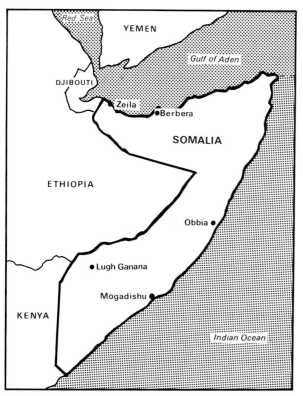

UGANDA

Uganda is an inland state in East Africa. The earliest people were Bantu-speaking farmers, ruled by a cattle-herding people called the Chwezi. The Chwezi (sometimes called Tutsi or Hima) came from the northeast and founded the kingdom of Kitara. It was invaded by another foreign group, the Luo, in about AD 1500.

The Luo were warriors from western

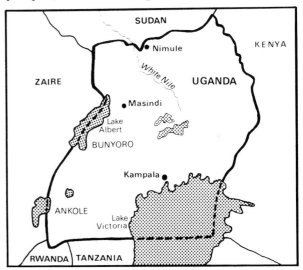

The last Kabaka of Buganda became Uganda's first president. He was deposed, and his kingdom was abolished in 1966.

small but prosperous, while Bunyoro shrank to a small state in the northwest, raided by slavers from Sudan. Bunyoro's northeastern neighbors were the Acholi and Alur people, cattle-herding Luo tribes.

Ethiopia attracted by the rich kingdom of Kitara, which was more advanced than their homeland. A Luo called Bito founded ruling families which reigned over the Bantu-speaking Bunyoro, Buganda, and Toro. The Chwezi were driven south into Ankole and even further into Rwanda and Burundi.

The Bito kingdoms flourished, especially Buganda. In about AD 1650 Buganda took over large areas of Bunyoro land. Buganda then took advantage of its Lake Victoria shore to trade with nearby states on the lake. When Arabs and Europeans brought guns into East Africa, Buganda bought them. The ruler, or Kabaka, of Buganda became the most powerful of the Ugandan kings. Toro and Ankole remained

In 1860-80 two new religions arrived. The Muslim faith came along the trade routes from the east coast. Christianity came with British missionaries, and it is now the dominant faith. The British government also took an interest. Britain controlled Egypt and did not want rival states controlling the source of the Nile River, which rises in Uganda. Britain established a protectorate in which the people were still ruled by their own kings, but they did so under British control.

In time the British wanted to link Uganda with the east coast, so they built a railway across Kenya, another British protectorate to the east.

Ugandan cash-crop farmers benefited

39

from the railway, but it did not make money right away, and Kenya had to maintain it. The coastal cities had many Indian businessmen and shopkeepers, and the railway brought many of them to Uganda. Many more Indians had been brought in to work on the railway, and they formed a large Indian communtiy.

The Uganda Protectorate ended in 1962. The independent state was to be a united republic, but the old kingdoms survived and there was no real unity. In 1966-67 the central government abolished the kingdoms, but the rivalry and local interests still go on. Tribal feelings have been particularly strong in the army. Therefore, there has been much violence in Uganda. English is the official language, but Kiswahili and many local languages are spoken.

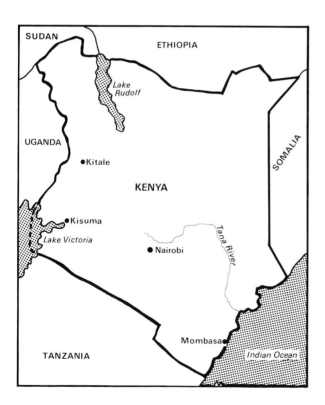

KENYA

Kenya is an East African country of great variety. The west is highland, the center is dry plain, and the coast has fertile crop land and big cities. The early people of the west were Bantu-speaking farmers. There were also the Luo, a herding people from further northeast who mingled with the Bantu villagers.

The northeast was often occupied by Galla and Somali nomads. There were also Bantu settlements of Kikuyu and Kamba farmers. Central Kenya was a vast range for the cattle of nomadic shepherds like the Masai. The Masai were not Bantu, because their language is one of a group from northeast Africa.

The different people moved about, shifting their homelands over long periods of time, and their ways of life affected each other. For instance, some of the Bantu tribes, who normally lived under a chief, copied the Masai system instead. This gave all men different grades of respect and responsibility according to their age.

Other Bantu speakers who settled on the coast band were affected by ideas from Arabia. Kenya, like Tanzania, had an Arab merchant class on the Indian Ocean shore. There was the same pattern of trade and contact with the inland people. The language of the coast was Swahili, a mixture of Bantu and Arabic.

The Arab sultan of Zanzibar became ruler of the coast as far north as the Tana River. His trading empire attracted not only Arabs but Indians, who traded all around the Indian Ocean. The sultan's power rested mainly on a profitable slave trade.

These houses, with grass roofs on a wooden framework, have not changed in style for centuries.

After 1822 the British began limiting the sultan's trade, so his power lessened as theirs grew. In 1888 the Imperial British East African Company was formed, and the company leased the coast from the sultan. The rest of Kenya became a British protectorate in 1895.

The British particularly wanted the fertile western highlands. The highlands appeared to be empty, and British settlers moved in. But the Masai and the local farmers had always spread into the highlands when they needed to. After a good year their numbers would increase, and they would need more land. But if there was hunger and their numbers fell, they withdrew again. The settlers on the highlands prevented this movement.

Trouble also arose over payment for labor. The settlers could not get enough labor. All they had to offer the local people was money, and local societies ran perfectly well without it. However, government also brought in taxes which had to be paid in money, so the natives had to work for the Europeans. This caused much resentment. The settlers felt they had been deceived about labor supplies, while the Africans felt that taxes which forced them to work were not much better than the slavery the British had put down.

There were also many Indians: merchant families and the workers the British had brought in to build the railway. All wanted more say in running Kenya.

In 1923 the British government set out a policy on African, settler, and Indian rights. The use of land remained the most difficult problem. In the 1950s it flared up again in terrorist uprisings among the Kikuyu.

Kenya became an independent country in 1963. The official language is Swahili, although English is widely used as well. The people are Muslim, Christian, Hindu, and animist.

CENTRAL AFRICAN REPUBLIC

The Central African Republic is a landlocked country north of the Congo River, with the Ubangi River flowing along its southern boundary.

The south is tropical rain forest. The first people to live there were the pygmies, some of whom still live in the southwest. After 1800 immigrants came from the north and northeast escaping from slave traders.

These refugees were mainly Baya from Chad and Banda from Sudan. They gradually spread through the northern savanna, through the wooded country, and into the forest. The tribes who settled near the Ubangi River became the most powerful, and there have been quarrels between them and the others ever since.

In 1910 the French made the area part of French Equatorial Africa. They organized diamond mining and rubber production, but access and transport were difficult. The country was a long way from the coast, and the big rivers provided the only routes through the forest. The impact of French ways was far less than in Senegal or Algeria.

France's rule ended in 1960, when the

Beads, feathers, and lion skins adorn dancers at M'Baiki in the Central African Republic.

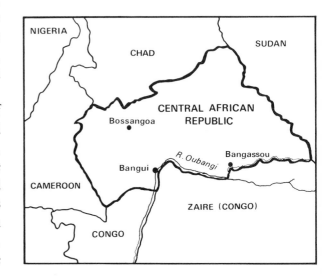

Republic was founded. In 1977 it became the Central African Empire when Jean Bedel Bokassa crowned himself emperor. He ruled for two years with much cruelty, but the country had kept links with France, and French forces eventually overthrew the emperor to restore the Republic.

French is still the official language, but Sango is most widely spoken. Christianity has spread to about a third of the people, while the rest are animist.

EQUATORIAL GUINEA

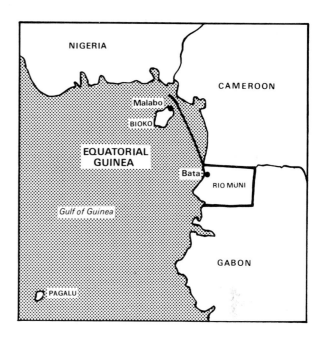

This small state on the west coast of central Africa has a mainland province called Rio Muni and two islands, Biyogo and Pagalu, to the northwest.

The early inhabitants were Bantu-speaking tribes. The Bubi people crossed to the islands; the Combe, Benga, and others lived on the coast; and the Fang lived inland. The mainland area is tropical, intensely hot, and dense jungle. The islands are cooler, and this is where the first European settlements were made. The Portuguese arrived on Pagalu in the fifteenth century and brought in slaves from the mainland. Their descendants still speak a dialect combining Portuguese and African elements.

It was the Spaniards, however, who became the rulers of what is now Equatorial Guinea. They replaced the Portuguese in 1778, but were not active until the British tried to set up a colony on one of the islands in 1827. The British wanted a settlement for newly freed slaves and for businessmen dealing with Nigeria.

The British occupation did not last long, but it was long enough for the merchants to make strong links with Nigeria. The Spanish government began encouraging settlers to establish plantations for cash crops. Workers were brought in from Nigeria.

Meanwhile, on the mainland the Fang had become powerful. They fought their way to the coast, defeating weaker tribes. The coast and island people had taken up Spanish customs and the Roman Catholic religion, but the Fang had a traditional tribal life and their own spirit worship. Their influence became stronger than Spain's.

Spanish rule ended in 1968, and Equatorial Guinea became an independent republic. In 1969 there was a short but violent civil war. Nigerian workers, Spaniards, and other non-Fang people left the country in large numbers. The Fang, on the other hand, have moved out farther to the islands. They share them with the descendants of Portuguese settlers and their slaves, of original Bubis, and of freed slaves settled by the British.

In a village deep in the Zaire jungle, local produce is displayed at a ramshackle market.

ZAIRE

Zaire is a vast country in central Africa. It is probably the early home of all the Bantu-speaking peoples. The Bantu are thought to have come from West Africa by using the rivers to travel through the thick forests. At Katanga, in southeastern Zaire, they found open land where they could settle. From there they colonized much of the continent, moving first into open land where farming or grazing was easy.

Some time after AD 300 food crops from the forests of southeastern Asia were brought to Africa by Asian immigrants to the east coast. The new root crops grew well in jungle clearings and enabled the Bantu to settle the jungles and forests of Zaire.

The jungle people lived in small, isolated villages. North and south of the jungles lay more open land. The people there grew grain, kept cattle, and mined copper and other precious metals. The jungle people did not join together and

form kingdoms, while the people on the open land did.

In the sixteenth century the Luba people formed a kingdom in south Zaire. It flourished west of them and was probably founded by Luba warlords. Ambitious warrior chiefs conquered many small chiefdoms until the Lunda empire stretched into Angola, and the Luba empire took tribute from chiefs far down the upper Congo River. Elsewhere were other groups of tribes: the Mongo and Kasai in the north and west, and the Kuba west of Luba.

The big kingdoms eventually broke up. The warlords who expanded them did not always stay obedient to the rulers of Luba and Lunda. By 1800 there were many small chiefdoms. When slavers from the east coast broke through to the Congo valley, no one was strong enough to stop them.

Many slave dealers were happy to take advantage of weak states and raid them. One who disagreed was Tippu Tib, an Arab. He thought the lack of firm rule in eastern Zaire was bad for business, and he decided to control the chiefdoms he dealt with. By 1870 he had an empire of his own reaching across to the Lomami River.

At that time European interest was growing. Explorers and missionaries had traveled the Congo returning with horrible stories of the slave trade. King Leopold of the Belgians began to make treaties with chiefs, until he had rights to develop over a million square miles of land. But the Congo was unhealthy, and Belgians did not want to settle there. Therefore the Belgian government was not interested in colonies. The king granted leases to Belgian companies to develop the land with local labor, but their treatment of their workers was appalling. By 1908 the Belgians were so horrified that the government took over the king's Congo Free State. The country produced diamonds, copper, coffee, palm oil, and rubber. European businessmen came to the Katanga highlands where the copper was mined, but the Belgian government kept control until independence came in 1960. This avoided the old problems with companies, but the people of Zaire had no chance to prepare for running their own country. There was no experienced leader whom all the different tribes would accept; therefore, there was civil war for five years.

Today about thirty-two million people live in Zaire. They speak more than two hundred languages, of which the most important are Lingala, Swahili, Tshiluba, and Kikongo. The official language is French. Roman Catholicism is well established, but many people are animists.

MOZAMBIQUE

Mozambique has a long coastline facing the Indian Ocean. Here two of the great African rivers, the Zambezi and the Limpopo, reach the sea. Because of these rivers, Mozambique has always attracted people who wanted to venture inland.

The native people are mainly Bantu-speaking, and the earliest arrivals came from Zambia and Zimbabwe in the Middle Ages. The Bantu speakers on the coast gradually adopted Swahili, a Bantu language mixed with Arabic. The Arabs were active traders on the coast and founded trading towns. The most important was Sofala, built in about AD 1200.

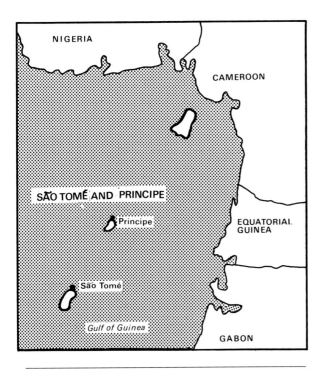

São Tomé also became a base for the trans-Atlantic slave trade. The island merchants bought slaves from mainland chiefs and shipped them to the Portuguese plantations in Brazil. In time, the islands' sugar plantations became less successful, and the islands lived mainly by trade until slavery was abolished in the nineteenth century.

Portuguese rule ended in 1975 when an independent republic was founded. Portuguese is the official language, and Roman Catholicism is the dominant religion.

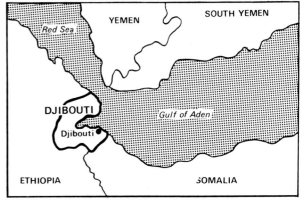

DJIBOUTI

Djibouti is a very small state on the coast of the Gulf of Aden in East Africa. The climate is harsh, and much of the country is semi-arid desert.

The towns on the coast have always been trading ports for Arab merchants. Pastoral people — Afars from Ethiopia and Issas from Somalia — use the small area inland for their herds.

Djibouti was held by France from 1884, when it became French Somaliland. The French wanted Djibouti because it was an

SÃO TOMÉ AND PRINCIPE

This very small country is a group of islands in the Gulf of Guinea, off the coast of Gabon. Both São Tomé and Principe are the main islands, but most of the people live on São Tomé.

The uninhabited islands were discovered by the Portuguese in 1471 and belonged to Portugal until 1975. At first the Portuguese used them as a base for their merchants trading on the coast of Nigeria. The islands were healthy for Europeans, while the Nigerian coast was not. Then it was found that sugar grew well on the islands. Settlers made plantations and brought in slaves from the nearby states of Nigeria, Congo, and Angola. These were the first Africans to live on the island.

outpost for the powerful kingdom of Ethiopia. They also wanted it because it lay at the southern end of the Red Sea. In 1884 this was the main route to the east for European shipping.

The French held Djibouti until 1977, when it became an independent republic.

Most people in Djibouti are Muslims because of the trading link with Arabia, where Islam began. The French introduced Roman Catholic Christianity, which still claims a few followers. The Afars and Issas have their own languages, but French and Arabic are also in use.

CAMEROON

Cameroon is in West Africa with a coastline on the Gulf of Guinea.

South Cameroon is tropical rain forest. Bantu-speaking blacks came here from Central Africa. Bete, Duala, Fang, Maka, and Ndjem were the major groups. They settled as farmers in forest clearings, where they grew root crops. In western Cameroon there are mountains. Those people also speak Bantu languages of a kind from the western coast of Africa. All these people had their own beliefs in spirits, magic, and the power of their ancestors.

The north was savanna country falling away to plains by Lake Chad. Farmers grew cereals, and there were also nomads. The northern people were not Bantu speakers. They were Sao, Fulani — a nomadic people found all over West Africa — and Kanuri from the eastern Sahara. The Muslim religion came through these northern people. In about 1810 the Muslim Fulani of northern Nigeria began a holy war which spilled over

Arab slavers in Cameroon lead their captives away in chains to the slave markets on the coast.

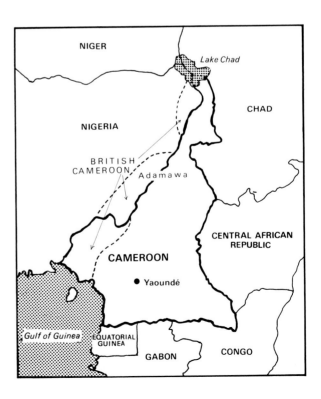

into northern Cameroon. There the Fulani founded a Muslim state called Adamawa.

By 1880 European merchants and Christian missionaries were active on the coast. Coastal Cameroon became a German protectorate in 1884. The Germans laid out cash-crop plantations in the south and began to work the forests. They had barely conquered the north, however, when they lost Cameroon to the British and French in World War I.

Cameroon was divided in 1919. The larger, eastern part was governed by France, and the smaller part in the west by Britain. In 1960 French Cameroon became an independent republic. In 1961 the people of British Cameroon voted on their future. Those of the north decided to join Nigeria, and the rest decided to join French Cameroon as one united, independent republic.

BOTSWANA

Botswana is in central southern Africa. It has a narrow belt of good land in the east, where most of the towns and villages are. North Botswana is hot and swampy, getting worse towards the Okavango basin. West Botswana is part of the Kalahari desert, a land of poor, dry soil, thorny bushes, and desert plants.

The first Botswana people were the Khoisan bush people, who still live in the Kalahari in small numbers. They survived by hunting small creatures that lived in the scrub and by gathering fruits and insects.

The Batswana (or Tswana) came later. They were Bantu-speaking farmers who lived in settled villages and small towns. They came from southeastern Zaire and

began to farm in eastern Botswana. Some of the local Khoisan people were attracted to this way of life, while others withdrew into the desert.

In the Middle Ages another Bantu-speaking group moved south through eastern Botswana. These were the Sotho people, who settled in parts of what is now South Africa. In the 1820s, however, they were forced to move because Zulu tribes were at war and the country was dangerous. Some Sotho moved into eastern Botswana. Those who went farthest north were the Ngwato, and their ruler was called the Khama.

In the 1850s the Khama had to cope with a number of foreign forces. There were warlike Ndebele next door, in what is now Zimbabwe. There were Dutch settlers from South Africa looking for new land. There were British mining companies looking for business, and British missionaries looking for converts.

The Ngwato used the British to fend off the others. Then in 1895 the British tried to join Botswana to their Cape of Good Hope colony, but the Khama and the other chiefs refused. Instead, the country became a British protectorate called Bechuanaland (an English attempt at Bakwena-land, after an important tribe called Bakwena). There were eight main tribes in the protectorate, and each looked after its own affairs.

The protectorate ended in 1966 when Botswana became an independent republic. Seretse Khama, chief of the Ngwato, was its first president. The official languages are Setswana and English, and Christianity is the main religion.

ANGOLA

Angola lies on the west coast of Central Africa, south of the Congo River. The Congo, or Kongo, kingdom used to cover part of northern Angola near the river mouth. This was a state of Bantu-speaking people, probably founded in the thirteeenth century AD. It was rich and flourishing when the Portuguese found it in 1482.

The Portuguese used the Kongo merchants' trading network and were able to influence the election of the Kongo kings. Their hold on Kongo and its slave trade lasted until about 1570.

By that time there were other powers in Angola. The kingdom of Ndongo lay south of Kongo and competed with it. Jaga warriors from Lubaland, in Zaire, attacked both kingdoms and set up their own military states between the Congo and the Cunene rivers. Another tribe, the Imbangala, conquered a kingdom for themselves in eastern Angola called Kasanje.

The Portuguese made a colony around Luanda in 1575. But they could not press

The flourishing Portuguese-built town of São Salvador in Angola is shown in this eighteenth-century engraving.

farther inland, and prospects of silver mines and rich farms had to be abandoned. They fell back on the slave trade and raided the Ndongo lands. Queen Nzinga (1624-63)

escaped with her people inland and founded a new kingdom called Matamba.

In time the Portuguese controlled Luanda and the old Ndongo kingdom. From there they conquered Kongo, which had turned against them. But they could not conquer Matamba, Kasanje, or the Jaga states. Instead, they traded with them.

In 1836 the Portuguese government banned the slave trade in Angola, although commercial trading lasted until 1950. The inland states were ruined, and the Portuguese settlers were left as the strongest power. Portuguese rule ended in 1975 after years of guerilla fighting for independence. Angola is now a one-party state.

The Portuguese introduced their Roman Catholic religion, which many people still follow, but most people are animists. Portuguese is still the official language. Other languages are Umbundu, Kimbundu, Lunda, and Kikongo.

SWAZILAND

Swaziland is a small country northeast of the Drakensberg Mountains of South Africa. The people were orginally Nguni. They came from Central Africa before AD 1600, and they settled in southern Swaziland in about 1800.

In the 1820s they moved again because of wars among the neighboring Zulu. The Nguni chief Sobhuza took his people farther north where it was safer. But the new settlement was still threatened by Zulus. In 1840 the chief asked the British government for protection.

At the same time the Dutch settlers of South Africa were moving ever farther north-

east from the Cape of Good Hope. During the reign of Sobhuza's son, Mswazi, the South Africans tried to take over Swaziland. The attempt did not succeed, but after that the future of Swaziland caused many disputes between Britain and South Africa. Afterward, Swaziland became a British protectorate in 1903.

The land was good and was divided between white settlers and Swazi people. The settlers held about 40% of the land. They used as plantations and ranches. The king remained head of state and ruled through his chiefs. The protectorate ended in 1968, and a fully independent kingdom was restored. The official language is English, but Siswati is used by almost all. Most people are Christians.

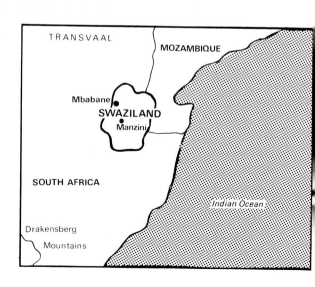

CONGO

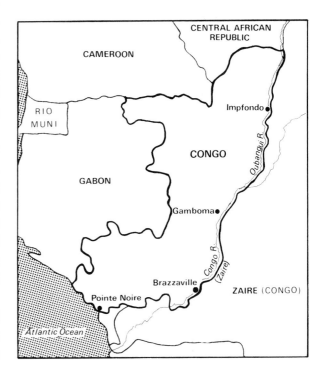

A group of slaves being branded before they are loaded onto ships on the Congolese coast.

Congo lies on the west coast of Central Africa, north of the lower Congo River. Most of the country is tropical rain forest. The settlers of the Middle Ages were Bantu-speaking blacks, who spread through the forest by river. They made clearings and grew food crops. Some of these farmers united their villages in small states.

On the southern coast and immediately inland there were three kingdoms: Kakongo, Loango, and Ngoyo. These states were the first to receive European traders in the fifteenth century. The trade was profitable for both sides. What the kingdoms could not offer themselves, they bought from people like the Teke further upriver and then resold.

European interest in the Congo increased until in the late nineteenth century French companies were granted leases on big areas of forest. The companies were interested in timber and rubber. They treated their workers badly and would have destroyed the farming life of the small tribes who did not wish to work for them or give up their land. In 1910 the French government took control, and Congo became part of French Equatorial Africa.

Congo became an independent republic in 1960, but the country still has links with France. About half the people belong to the Roman Catholic Church and the rest are animist. French is the official language, but everyday languages are Kongo, Teke, Sango, and Ubangi.

ZAMBIA

Zambia is an inland country in southern Africa, north of the Zambezi River. The early people moved down from Katanga in southern Zaire. They were Bantu-speaking tribes who lived by various kinds of farming. The Tongo and Ila people in the south were grain growers and cattle herders. They did not have kings or important chiefs. The Lozi kingdom was founded in the seventeenth century on the plain around the Zambezi. The first Lozi kings were probably warlords from Zaire. The kings of Kazembe, a northwestern kingdom, certainly were. They were sent east in the eighteenth century to conquer land for the ruler of the Lunda empire. The highlands they found were fertile, rich in copper, and well placed for trade. Therefore, they were able to become powerful and independent.

The riches of Kazembe tempted Nyamwezi merchants from Tanganyika who setttled there after 1800. Slave traders from Zanzibar also came. In the 1860s the Nyamwezi settlers broke away to found a kingdom of their own. The two kingdoms became rivals and were both weakened. The slave traders took advantage of this. When British missionaries came to the Lozi kingdom they were horrified by the slaving raids. They hoped that their Christian teachings would stamp out slavery and that British businessmen would be able to introduce a new economy to replace the slave trade. In the 1880s, the British South Africa Company arrived, led by Cecil Rhodes, and bought mining rights from the kings, hoping that the country was rich in minerals. The company was soon the biggest power in the land, which became known as Northern Rhodesia. It ran the country until it became a British protectorate in 1924. Only after that did the great mineral wealth appear.

In the 1930s it was realized how valuable the copper mines in Kazembe could be. Mining began on a large scale. During the next twenty years this area — called the

Copperbelt — acquired a big, mixed population and many Europeans. Northern Rhodesia became a rich country.

The Europeans wanted union with Southern Rhodesia, which was also run by white settlers. Nobody else did. The union existed for ten years but was not a success. Northern Rhodesia withdrew in 1963 and became independent as Zambia in 1964. The official language is English, and Christianity is the dominant religion.

LESOTHO

Lesotho is a small kingdom in the Drakensberg Mountains, completely surrounded by South Africa. (See map on page 58.)

The kingdom was founded in 1818. At that time there were wars among the Zulus of northeastern South Africa, and the Sotho people were driven from their homelands by the fighting. A chief called Moshoeshoe led his people to safety in the mountains. Other refugees followed, and a small state was formed.

The area was still dangerous. There were Zulu armies out for conquest, and there was conflict between British and Dutch settlers. In 1868 Moshoeshoe put his kingdom under British protection. The British called it Basutoland, from "Ba-Sotho-land."

The protectorate lasted until 1966 when the country became a fully independent kingdom. The people speak Sesotho, but English is also used. British missionaries introduced the Christian faith, to which about two-thirds of the people belong.

ZIMBABWE

Zimbabwe is a republic in southern Africa. The Zambezi River flows along the northwestern boundary, and the Limpopo River flows along the south. Most of the country is a big plateau rising to hills.

The first powerful people were the Shona, who still live there. They founded the rich kingdom of Great Zimbabwe, which flourished until about AD 1400. The people mined gold and copper that they sold to the coastal cities of what is now Mozambique. The merchants of the coast were Arabs and Swahili-speaking Africans. They came up the Zambezi and Mazoe rivers to big markets in the northwest, where some of them settled.

In about 1400 the Shona people left Great Zimbabwe and moved to the northwest themselves. There they founded a new kingdom called Mwene Matapa. This was the kingdom the Portuguese found when they explored the Arab trade routes

after 1500. The southwest part of Mwene Matapa broke away in about 1490 and became the kingdom of Butwa. Mwene Matapa grew weaker as the Portuguese increased their hold on it, while Butwa grew stronger. By about 1700 the Butwa kingdom had forced most of the Portuguese explorers and traders out and firmly controlled those who were left.

After 1835 there was an invasion from the south. Wars among tribes of northern South Africa forced some chiefs to move away to seek new homelands. The Nguni marched through Butwa on their way north and left it so weak that it was conquered by the next wave of southern adventurers, the Ndebele. By 1880 the Ndebele were joined by the Shona.

At that time there was great rivalry in South Africa between British and Dutch settlers. The Dutch kept moving north to escape British rule, but the British wanted to be first in any northern country where there might be minerals or good land. The British South Africa Company, headed by Cecil Rhodes, bought mining rights and made treaties among the Shona and Ndebele. But there were arguments as to what had been agreed. The company then took over the Shona land and conquered the Ndebele between 1893 and 1897. These two areas and land to the north of them (now Zambia) were called Rhodesia. Settlers were invited from England and South Africa.

The country was not as rich in minerals as Rhodes had hoped, so the settlers wanted to farm instead. This meant moving on to large areas of land that Shona and Ndebele farmers did not want to give up. There was fighting in 1896-97.

In 1923 the British government took over Rhodesia from the company. The first government of this British colony was made up only of settlers. The settlers felt that their money and hard work was making the country prosperous, so they should decide its future. The British government believed its own civil servants were more likely to be fair to everybody. The Shona and the Ndebele nationalist groups felt that they were being kept out of the running of their own country. The disagreements grew worse, until Southern Rhodesia declared itself independent in 1965 with a settler government. Nationalists then took to guerilla war. This lasted until 1979 when the settlers lost their overall control.

Rhodesia was recognized as an independent republic in 1980 and changed its name to Zimbabwe. There are still differences, and sometimes violence, between the followers of Shona and Ndebele leaders. English is the official language with Shona and Ndebele widely spoken. Animism and Christianity are the main faiths.

MALAWI

Malawi is a small country lying west and south of Lake Malawi in southern Africa. The name comes from Maravi, a kingdom south of the lake which outsiders first discovered in about AD 1500. Maravi legends tell how the first kings came from the Luba empire in Zaire. Most of the people then were Cewa, but many different immigrants came in the nineteenth century.

From Tanganyika, Yao slavers and ivory hunters moved into the highlands south of the lake. Eventually they crossed the lake and settled as traders on the western shore. In 1835, Nguni warriors came north from what is now South Africa. They had been driven from their home by war, and had to find and settle a new homeland. Small Nguni states grew up in Malawi.

The Yao and Nguni between them broke up the Maravi empire. They were followed by slave traders from the east coast — Arabs and Swahili-speaking Africans who found the country in such chaos that they were able to win control of many chiefdoms.

In 1858 the British missionary David Livingstone set out to explore the Zambezi River. He was unable to get further than the falls at Kabra Basa, so he turned north and followed the Shire River into Malawi instead. Livingstone thought the highlands of southern Malawi would suit Europeans, and more British missionaries and traders arrived in the 1870s and 1880s. They wanted to end slave trading and build up other trades instead. They needed government support to do this, and the British made Malawi a protectorate in 1891 with the name of Nyasaland.

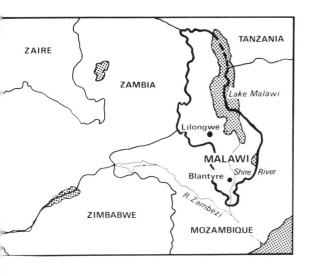

In Malawi a peasant farmer uses a primitive tool to clear mud and stones out of an irrigation ditch.

Malawi became a republic in 1964. About six million people live there today. They speak Bantu, mainly Chichewa, but English is the official language. Most people are animist, with Christian, Muslim, and Hindu minorities.

SOUTH AFRICA

South Africa is the southernmost African state. It includes two small islands — Prince Edward and Marion in the Indian Ocean, and the Walvis Bay enclave in Namibia.

The early people were the San, or Bushmen, who lived by hunting and gathering wild food. There were also the Khoi-khoi, or Hottentots, who were nomadic shepherds. Archaeologists have found evidence

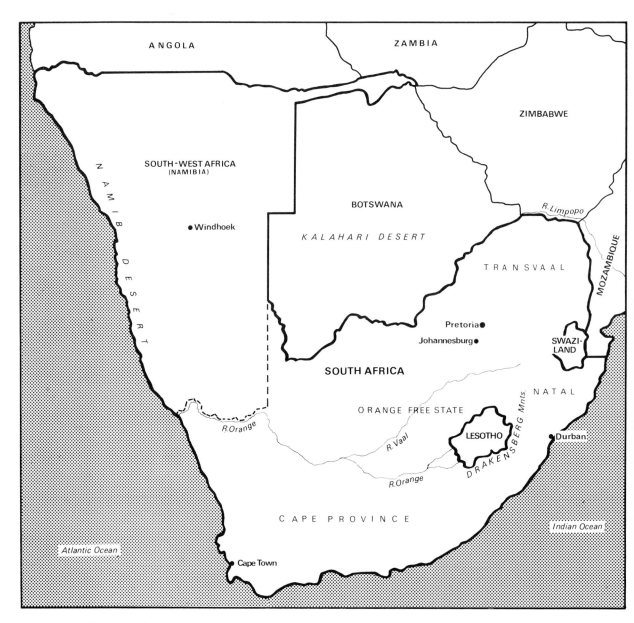

of the first blacks who migrated to South Africa. This evidence has been dated to around AD 250. The origins of these early peoples are uncertain.

These settlers had some cattle but lived mainly by growing crops. South Africa gets its rain from the winds of the Indian Ocean. Therefore it is wettest in the east and gets drier towards the west. The crop-growing people, settling down to cultivate one place, needed better rainfall than the hunters and the nomads who moved on to fresh pasture when they needed to. So the first farmers stayed in the east between the Drakensberg Mountains and the sea. Groupings into the tribes of today (such as Sotho, Nguni, etc.)

probably occurred long after arrival.

The first Europeans to explore the coast were the Portuguese in 1488. Their power was ended by the Dutch in about 1610. The Dutch East India Company wanted a base for their ships on the way to the spice-growing lands of the Far East, and in 1652 they founded Cape Town. Cape Town grew, and its people had to be fed. The surrounding land was good and unlike most of the west, had enough rain. Dutch settlers were invited in. The proud Khoi-khoi pastoralists could not be induced to work for the newcomers. This made food expensive, so the Company brought in slave labor from Asia and other African countries.

The settlement outgrew its land. Farming families moved into the interior to begin cattle ranching. Like the Khoi-khoi, they found that they had to cover great distances to get enough pasture. This competition for land by the gunpowder-owning Dutch settlers virtually destroyed the Khoi-khoi. When the traveling farmer (*trekboer* in Dutch) moved farther east and found good crop land, however, he came up against much tougher opposition.

The Dutch settlers, called Afrikaners, still inhabited the Cape colony. They had been pushing its frontiers out as they went. By the end of the eighteenth century they were trying to settle among the Africans of the east. The native Africans already fought each other over rights to land, but now they fought the Afrikaners as well, and the new frontiers were always at risk.

Between 1795 and 1802 and from 1806 the colony fell to the British. The new British government tried to control the far-away Afrikaner settlers and to defend the

A battle at the Intombi River during the Zulu War of 1879, drawn by a soldier who took part.

new frontiers, which were always being attacked.

The Afrikaners often got along with new British settlers quite well. However, the Afrikaners and the British government never got along, and there was constant disagreement. When slavery was abolished the Afrikaners felt cheated over proper compensation. British missionaries arrived in the frontier lands and criticized the Afrikaner view of Africans as un-Christian.

Throughout the nineteenth century the Afrikaners kept moving on to escape British rule. That rule followed them into the new province of Natal, but they did succeed in setting up their own states of Transvaal and the Orange Free State.

The Afrikaners were also involved in wars with the Nguni, particularly a northern group called the Zulu. From about 1820 the Zulu were at war with their Nguni neighbors. Huge areas of land emptied as the people fled. The Afrikaners moved in, thinking the land unoccupied. The Zulu attacked, and the Afrikaners in the end defeated them. But then the Nguni refugees moved back because the danger was over, and there was still more dispute as to whose land it was.

In 1886 the bigest gold field in the world was found in the Transvaal. The Afrikaner states now had wealth. Disagreements between them and the British developed into a struggle for control of South Africa. War broke out in 1899. The British sent out powerful armies, and inevitably the two Afrikaner republics were conquered. But many people in Britain disapproved of the war and thought it wrong that the Afrikaner states should become British colonies. In 1910, new British leadership and South Africans like Jan Smuts united all the old British and Afrikaner settlements in the new, independent Union of South Africa.

The European settlers were never prepared to regard non-whites as citizens entitled to equal rights. This attitude hardened during British rule and early independence. By 1948 it had become formalized in the policy of apartheid — separate rules and laws for each racial group, necessitating forced removals of blacks to largely unproductive areas and restrictions on many social and commercial activities. Various homelands were set up, of which Transkei, Ciskei, Bophuthatswana, and Venda opted for independence. There is great agitation for change, and despite some recent changes, apartheid remains the country's most difficult problem.

Namibia is a big state in southwestern Africa. The name comes from the Namib desert which runs along the coast. The Kalahari desert covers much of the north and east. The people are Ovambo (Bantu-speaking farmers), Hereros (shepherds), Nama (thought to come from northeast

San trackers with bows and arrows in the Namibian desert. The San are the earliest people of southernmost Africa.

Jan Van Riebeeck lands at the Cape to establish the first Dutch settlement in South Africa.

Africa), and San of the Kalahari. The San are the original people who once lived by hunting and gathering wild food. Now, many have settled to farm and herd.

Namibia became a German colony after 1884. The Germans lost it to South African forces during World War I. After the war the South African government managed Namibia, but the Ovambo and other tribes do not want to live under South African rule. Since 1966 there have been several outbreaks of war.

The official languages of South Africa and Namibia are English and Afrikaans, but several African languages are widely spoken, as is German in Namibia. The dominant religion is Christianity.

ST. HELENA

St. Helena is an island in the Atlantic Ocean about 1,200 miles (1,920 km) west of southern Angola. It has been a British colony since 1834. It has two dependencies of its own: Ascension, a small island approximately 700 miles (1,120 km) to the northwest, and Tristan da Cunha, a group of islands (Tristan, Gough, Inaccessible, and Nightingale) in the mid-Atlantic. Most of the people are of British descent.

GLOSSARY

Afrikaner: A person born in South Africa of white parents, usually of Dutch descent, whose language is Afrikaans, South African Dutch.

Animism: A religion based on the belief that the universe and all natural things have souls or spirits. It is sometimes called spirit worship.

Bantu: A large family of tribes in central and southern Africa whose languages come from the same language family.

Bedouins: Nomadic tribes brought into North Africa from Arabia by the Arabs around 1050. The Arab rulers hoped they would tame the Bedouins and the Berbers, but instead the two mingled to become the Tuareg tribes.

Berbers: The native nomadic desert tribes of North Africa.

Colony: A country or people ruled or settled by a foreign power.

Coptic Church: The native Christian church of Egypt.

Islam: Religion founded by Mohammed in Arabia in the seventh century AD whose followers are called Muslims. Islam has spread throughout much of Africa.

League of Nations: An organization formed after World War I to promote peace. It was replaced by the United Nations.

Missionaries: People who go to foreign lands and try to convert the people there to their own religion.

Nomads: Races or tribes with no fixed home, who move from place to place in search of food.

Persian Empire: An ancient empire that once stretched from Egypt to India.

Phoenicians: People from an ancient country on the east coast of the Mediterranean. They were famous sea traders.

Protectorate: A weak state under the protection of a strong state that controls it wholly or partially.

Republic: A state with an elected head of government. Supreme power rests with those citizens who are entitled to vote.

Roman Empire: An empire set up by Romans in the first century BC ruling parts of North Africa.

Turkish Empire: An empire founded by the Turks in about AD 1300 that included a large area of North Africa. It collapsed after World War I.

Turks: Turkic-speaking peoples from Turkestan who founded the Seljuk and Ottoman empires.

United Nations: A group of nations formed after World War II to promote world peace and cooperation.

World War I (1914 - 18): A war fought by the United States, Canada, Britain, and their allies against Germany, Austria-Hungary, Turkey, and their allies. Germany and Turkey lost African territories after defeat in this war.

World War II (1939 - 45): A war between Britain, France, the Soviet Union, the United States, and their allies against Germany, Italy, Japan, and their allies. It was fought partly in Africa.

Picture Acknowledgments — Bodleian Library 5; De Beers Consolidated Mines 13, 44; Documentation Francaise 42; Egyptian Embassy, London 33; Mansell Picture Library 39; Mary Evans Picture Library 10, 26, 51; Namibia Department of Education 60; National Museum, Lagos 8; Nigerian High Commission, London 28; Oxfam (MAL 14.15) 57; Rowntree-Mackintosh 4; South African Library 61; Richard Steel 41; Sara Steel 17, 34, 37, 59; Town Docks (153771), 23 (152898 Kay Muldoon), 24 (152872), 32 (153811).